Improving Foreign Language Speaking through Formative Assessment

Harry Grover Tuttle, Ed. D.
Alan Robert Tuttle

D1279649

Routledge
Taylor & Francis Group
New York London

First published 2012 by Eye On Education

Published 2013 by Routledge
711 Third Avenue, New York, NY 10017, USA
2 Park Square, Milton Park, Abingdon, Oxon OX14 4RN

Routledge is an imprint of the Taylor & Francis Group, an informa business

Library of Congress Cataloging-in-Publication Data

Tuttle, Harry Grover.
Improving foreign language speaking through formative assessment/
Harry Grover Tuttle and Alan Robert Tuttle.
    p.   cm.
Includes bibliographical references.
ISBN 978-1-59667-197-3
1. Language and languages—Study and teaching.
2. Second language acquisition.
3. Language and languages—Ability testing.
I. Tuttle, Alan Robert.
II. Title.
P51.T88 2011
418.0071—dc23   2011025019

Cover Designer: Dave Strauss, 3FoldDesign

ISBN: 978-1-596-67197-3 (pbk)

Also Available from EYE ON EDUCATION

Successful Student Writing Through Formative Assessment
Harry Grover Tuttle

Formative Assessment: Responding to Your Students
Harry Grover Tuttle

Teacher-Made Assessments:
How to Connect Curriculum, Instruction, and Student Learning
Christopher R. Gareis & Leslie W. Grant

Teaching, Learning, and Assessment Together:
Reflective Assessments for Elementary Classrooms
Arthur K. Ellis

A Good Start:
147 Warm-Up Activities for Spanish Class (Un Buen Comienzo)
Rebekah Stathakis

Activities, Games, and Assessment Strategies
for the Foreign Language Classroom
Amy Buttner

Differentiated Instruction:
A Guide for Foreign Language Teachers
Deborah Blaz

100 Games and Activities
for the Introductory Foreign Language Classroom
Thierry Boucquey

A Collection of Performance Tasks and Rubrics:
Foreign Languages
Deborah Blaz

Short Cycle Assessment:
Improving Student Achievement through Formative Assessment
Susan Lang, Todd Stanley, & Betsy Moore

Dedication

This book is dedicated to all students who take a modern foreign language with the desire to be speakers of the language. Hopefully, their teachers will use formative assessment to help them become good communicators in their target languages.

About The Authors

Dr. Harry Grover Tuttle has been awarded the Ruth E. Wasley Distinguished Teacher Award by the New York State Association of Foreign Language Teachers. He was part of a foreign language program recognized as one of the fifty most innovative in the United States. He has taught at the college level and at the sixth grade through Advance Placement; also, Dr. Tuttle has taught English as a second language at many colleges. He has been active in many professional organizations such as the American Council of Teaching of Foreign Languages (ACTFL), American Association of Teachers of Spanish and Portuguese, New York State Association of Foreign Language Teachers, and Foreign Language Association of Central New York. Harry has published in ACTFL's *Foreign Language Annals, Hispania, Spanish Today, TESOL Quarterly, International Society for Technology in Education, SIGTC Connections, New York State Association of Foreign Language Teachers Journal, and TechLearning*. In addition to writing several articles for various publications, Dr. Tuttle has written five books including *Formative Assessment: Responding to Your Students* and *The World in Your Classroom: Global Education in Language Learning*.

Alan Robert Tuttle has taught at the high school level (Grade 9 through Advanced Placement) and at Cedarville University and Indiana University. He is pursuing his Master of Arts in Teaching at Indiana University. Alan has been an AP reader. He has traveled to Spain three times.

Acknowledgments

We wish to acknowledge those who helped us develop our ideas about foreign language teaching.

Harry thanks Beth Hemkes, Shirley Sherburne-Zimmer, Robert Sherburne, Anthony Papalia, the language teachers at North Syracuse Central Schools, the Foreign Language Association of Central New York (FLACNY), the New York State Association of Foreign Language Teachers (NYSAFLT), and the American Council on the Teaching of Foreign Languages (ACTFL). In addition, Harry thanks his wife, Joellyn Tuttle, for her support.

Alan thanks all of his Spanish teachers: Sr. Norton, Sr. Morales, Sra. Craig, Dra. Loach, Andrés, Juan Miguel, and Professor Power for their instruction and guidance. Alan would also like to thank his father (his co- author), his mother Joellyn, and his wife, Sarah, for their constant support and encouragement.

We also wish to thank those educators who either used these formative assessments with their students or provided valuable feedback during the preparation of this book: Robert Manipole, Lynn Kauffman, Anthony J. Madonia, Valerie Valero, Melody Mariani, Gail Sullivan, Helene Zimmer-Loew, and Joellyn Tuttle.

We thank Robert Sickles and Lauren Beebe, our editors.

Free Downloads

Many of the tools discussed and displayed in this book are also available on the Routledge website as Adobe Acrobat files. Permission has been granted to purchasers of this book to download these tools and print them.

You can access these downloads by visiting www.routledge.com/9781596671973 and click on the Free Downloads tab.

Index of Free Downloads

Table of Contents

Preface

This is as a how-to book on using formative assessment in the foreign language classroom, with many practical suggestions for the classroom teacher. Although teachers are the primary audience of this book, principals, curriculum leaders, and pre-service educators will also find it a useful guide to formative assessment. Public school teachers as well as college professors have used the activities from this book to enable students to show improvements in their speaking as they climb the American Council on the Teaching of Foreign Languages (ACTFL) Proficiency Guidelines (1999). You can use these techniques with very little, if any, modifications.

Although numerous formative assessment experts, such as Douglas Reeves, Larry Ainsworth, Rick Stiggins, Paul Black and Dylan Wiliam, W. James Popham, and Grant Wiggins, focus on national, state, or district-wide efforts, this book supports teachers such as yourself at the classroom level. As much as we have relied on the writings of formative assessment experts, we have also relied on the experiences of schools and teachers who are implementing a formative assessment approach to speaking in the classroom. Because continuous growth is an important aspect of formative assessment, your students will grow in their speaking from one speaking assessment to another (Ainsworth & Viegut, 2007). Likewise, according to formative assessment, each of your students' speaking assessments will show improvement over the previous speaking.

Your students will take many short formative speaking assessments instead of just one long summative assessment at the end of a chapter; each formative assessment will help the students improve. These smaller, informal assessments help your students be successful before they take a summative assessment. As you select a language function from Part 3, you can monitor your students, diagnose any learning gaps, have peers give formative feedback, and, if necessary, you can show struggling students a wide variety of strategies to overcome their difficulties. Your focus will be on your students' continuous speaking improvement.

Part 1: Assessing and Improving Speaking identifies current speaking assessment practices and explains the need for formative assessment.

Part 2: Formative Assessment Overview provides an introduction to formative assessment with explanations and examples of monitoring, diagnosing, giving feedback, providing time to grow, reporting growth, and celebrating success. This overview includes a section on grading within formative assessment and a section on transforming your present classroom speaking activities into formative assessments.

Part 3: Speaking Formative Assessments incorporate the theory of formative assessment into a multitude of actual oral proficiency formative assessments. This assessment section includes the format of the assessment, the assessment form, speaking topics, and formative strategies for improvement. Peers assess each other and, if needed, the teacher will provide additional learning strategy support. Each language function has an average of ten strategies that you can give the students to help them overcome speaking gaps. If you are already familiar with formative assessment theory, you can go immediately to this third section for the specifics on using it in your classroom.

We are confident that, as you implement these formative assessment techniques, you will notice improvement in your students' speaking as they move through the ACTFL Proficiency Guidelines.

1

Assessing and Improving Speaking

Speaking Goals

According to a report from the Office for Standards in Education (2008), children studying foreign languages have poor speaking skills despite improvements in the quality of teaching and learning. At all levels, the report found that speaking was the least developed of pupils' skills and that pupils' inability to express themselves had a negative impact on their confidence and enthusiasm. Students who have an A grade in language classes often cannot communicate in the language. Students who take a language class often complain to their friends or family members that they cannot speak the language. Bailey (2005) reports that speaking intuitively seems to be the most important of language skills because people who know a language are referred to as a "speaker" of the language as though speaking included all other skills.

The American Council on the Teaching of Foreign Language (ACTFL) promotes language skills in the United States. In 1996, a collaboration of four national language associations including ACTFL, American Association of Teachers of French (AATF), American Association of Teachers of German (AATG), and American Association of Teachers of Spanish (AATSP) developed five major goals of language study: Communication, Cultures, Connections, Comparisons, and Communities (1998). These goals interweave so that any one goal incorporates parts of the other goals. In the Communication goal, there are three standards and three modes.

- ◆ "Standard 1.1: Students engage in conversations, provide and obtain information, express feelings and emotions, and exchange opinions" (interpersonal mode).
- ◆ "Standard 1.2: Students understand and interpret written and spoken language on a variety of topics" (interpretative mode).

- "Standard 1.3: Students present information, concepts, and ideas to an audience of listeners or readers on a variety of topics" (presentational mode). (Communication, Cultures, Connections, Comparisons, and Communities, 1998)

This book of speaking strategies focuses mainly on assessing an individual as he/she speaks.

Language learning has been transformed from learning about a language to actually speaking a language. ACTFL has moved from seat-time guidelines to proficiency-based guidelines. The ACTFL Proficiency Guidelines of 1999 establishes what it means to be proficient at the Superior, Advanced, Intermediate, and Novice levels (Breiner-Sanders, Lowe, Miles & Swender, 2000):

Superior-level speakers are characterized by the ability to:

- Communicate with accuracy and fluency to participate fully and effectively in conversations on a variety of topics in formal and informal settings from both concrete and abstract perspectives. They can just as easily talk about their meal as a social or political issue. They satisfy the linguistic demands of professional and/or scholarly life.
- Explain matters in detail, providing lengthy and coherent narrations, all with ease, fluency, and accuracy. They explain their opinions and construct and develop hypotheses to explore alternative possibilities.
- Command a variety of interactive and discourse strategies such as turn-taking and separating main ideas from supporting ones through the use of syntactic and lexical devices, as well as intonational features such as pitch, stress, and tone.

Advanced-level speakers are characterized by the ability to:

- Perform with linguistic ease, confidence, and competence. They discuss topics concretely and abstractly. They participate actively in formal exchanges on a variety of concrete topics such as work, school, home, leisure activities, as well as events of current, public, and personal interest or relevance.
- Narrate and describe in major time frames with good control of aspect.
- Provide a structured argument to explain and defend opinions and develop effective hypotheses within extended discourse.
- Use communication strategies such as paraphrasing, circumlocution, and illustration.
- Use precise vocabulary and intonation.

Intermediate-level speakers are characterized by the ability to:

- ◆ Converse with ease and confidence when dealing with the most routine tasks and social situations. Handle many uncomplicated tasks and social situations requiring an exchange of basic information related to work, school, recreation, particular interests, self, family, home, and daily activities, as well as physical and social needs such as food, shopping, travel, and lodging.
- ◆ Narrate and describe in major time frames using connected discourse of paragraph length; however, they cannot maintain the narration and demonstrate weaknesses in their narration.
- ◆ Obtain and give information by asking and answering questions to obtain simple information to satisfy basic needs.

Novice-level speakers are characterized by the ability to:

- ◆ Handle uncomplicated communicative tasks in straightforward social situations. They respond to simple questions on the predictable topics necessary for survival in the target language culture such as basic personal information, basic objectives, and a limited number of preferences or requests for information.
- ◆ Convey minimal meaning by using isolated words and short, sometimes incomplete sentences. They use lists of words, memorized phrases and some personalized combinations of words and phrases.
- ◆ Ask only a few formulaic questions. (Breiner-Sanders, Lowe, Miles & Swender, 2000)

ACTFL has determined that by the end of the students' first year of language learning, such as ninth grade or the combination of seventh and eighth grade, they can reach the middle of the Novice level (Figure 1.1, page 6). As they continue their second and third year of language study, they may reach the Intermediate level. Some students who take Advanced Placement or the equivalent begin to reach the lower levels of the Advanced (1998).

Speaking Assessments

Due to the increased emphasis on speaking, many language tests incorporate a speaking component. ACTFL's Oral Proficiency Interview, Center for Applied Linguistics' Simulated Oral Proficiency Interview, ACTFL's Integrated Performance Assessment, the Advanced Placement test, and school district language finals represent a few assessments that include speaking a target language.

FIGURE 1.1 ACTFL Levels and Grade Levels

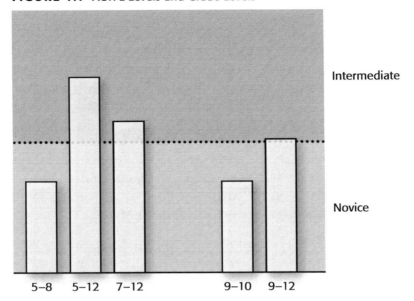

In each speaking assessment, students perform an oral task and receive a level or a score. To illustrate, a student may respond with four sentences to a prompt situation such as agreeing with his friend (the teacher) on what they are going to do together this weekend. He may receive a score such as 4/6.

These oral assessments are final or summative assessments. These tests inform the students where they are in general terms with a final score or rating such as a "5" on the Advanced Placement exam. These tests do not help the students understand their specific strengths and areas for improvement. More importantly, they do not provide the students with strategies to become better speakers. Furthermore, the students take these speaking tests separately from classroom learning. These summative speaking assessments are not a natural part of the class. Additionally, the students take the same speaking assessment only once. They do not learn new strategies and then retake the assessment to show their growth over time. Finally, these one-time speaking assessments are high-stakes tests which create a great deal of student anxiety (Tuttle, 2009). Formative assessment overcomes these negatives of summative speaking tests.

You, along with your language colleagues, may have developed your own variations of assessments to test students' speaking with your own rubrics or check lists. Buttner (2007) includes numerous ways in which she and others assess speaking such as "Essential Questions" and "Dialogue and Role Play Rubric." These rubrics identify where the students are in the speaking process. Assessment tools need to identify specific speaking skills, not just a general skill category like "Completeness of response" and its vague

FIGURE 1.2 Vague Summative Speaking Rubric (Partial)

	4: Above Proficient	3: Proficient	2: Developing	1: Beginning
Completeness of Response	Extremely complete	Generally complete	Sometimes complete	Incomplete

four-point scale (Figure 1.2). For example, in a formative assessment rubric the general category of "Completeness of response" includes specific critical sub-skills and the teacher writes in a specific strategy to help the student improve (Figure 1.3, page 8).

If you use speaking rubrics that do not offer improvement strategies to the students, then the assessments remain summative. Formative assessment rubrics not only indicate the students' strengths and areas for improvement, but also provide a concrete strategy to move the students forward in their speaking skills. If you do not offer the students any strategy for their improvement, they remain stuck in their present learning gaps and they are unlikely to show improvement from one assessment to the next. If coaches do not provide any strategies for improvement for their athletes during the season, their teams will not get better. If a person uses the wrong fingering for a piano piece for many hours, the person does not become a better musician.

Formative assessment embeds the oral evaluation into the normal classroom activities. These evaluations do not take time away from normal instruction since they are a natural outgrowth of the instruction. Also, formative assessment encourages peer review so that the whole class can be working in pairs to assess each other. Students have more opportunities to talk for extended periods of time with these formative assessments. When students evaluate each other in specific objective ways, such as determining if the partner gives information and opinions about a topic, they provide very good growth feedback to their partners. Growth happens when speaking is assessed on a frequent basis through formative assessment.

Although you may not formally assess often, you informally evaluate the oral proficiency of your students on a daily basis when you call on them in class. You react to their language successes and language problems as they occur. Omaggio Hadley (2001) reported several types of in-class speaking error correction teachers use:

- ◆ **Explicit correction**. Give the correct form to students and tell them what they said was incorrect. *Example*: Student says, "Yesterday I speak"; you respond, "Spoke. Speak is wrong."
- ◆ **Recast**. Rephrase student's utterances to eliminate error. *Example*: Student says, "Yesterday I speak"; you respond, "Yesterday I spoke."

FIGURE 1.3 Formative Speaking Rubric (Partial)

	4: Above Proficient	3: Proficient	2: Developing	1: Beginning
Completeness of Response	• answers the basic question and gives additional information/details (Ex: For the question of "Where does Nico swim?" also tells when he swims, how often he swims, what the lake is like, describes the weather, etc.)	• answers the basic question • answers the specific question word (answers "Where does Nico swim?" with a place such as "He swims in a lake.") • gives specific information ("He swims in Cayuga Lake.") • answers in a complete sentence	• partially answers the question • uses a word or phrase such as "Cayuga Lake" instead of a full sentence • answers with a general, unspecific answer, such as "in a lake"	• does not answer the question • May not: understand the question word, understand the question, know how to answer the question word or the question, know how to form the answer, have enough vocabulary, know the answer
Strategy for improvement based on student's speaking:				

- ♦ **Clarification requests**. Implicit correction in which you indicate that you did not understand the student by saying something like "Pardon?"
- ♦ **Metalinguistic feedback**. Comment or ask questions about the form of the students' utterance without explicitly correcting it. *Example*: Student says, "Yesterday I speak." You ask, "Did you say 'speak'?"
- ♦ **Elicitation**. Try to get the student to produce the correct form either by completing your own restatement, asking the student questions about how something should be said, or asking the student to repeat the utterance in a reformulated version. *Example*: Student says, "Yesterday I speak." You respond, "Today I speak, Yesterday I. . . ."
- ♦ **Raising tone**. Repeat the incorrect utterance with rising intonation or emphasis so that the student knows which part is in need of repair. *Example*: Student says, "Yesterday I speak. You respond, "Yesterday I speak" (rising intonation).

According to Omaggio Hadley's review of the research of Lyster and Ranta (2001, p. 268), recast is the most commonly used teacher technique. They report that this technique is relatively ineffective as a means of getting students to repair their own speech. Students find recast somewhat ambiguous since they probably do not know if the teacher is responding to the content or the form of what they are saying. In recasting, the students know that they just have to repeat what the teacher says, even if they do not understand it. Simply repeating the sentence does not help the students identify the present learning gap, does not provide them with a specific strategy for overcoming the gap, and does not allow them time to improve once they have learned how to overcome the gap. The other forms of error correction demonstrate these same weaknesses. On the other hand, formative assessment can raise the students' speaking achievement. It identifies the students' specific gap, such as not saying details in order to elaborate on a topic; it provides a strategy to overcome it, such as saying different verbs in each sentence; and it allows students to practice that strategy to show success (Black & Jones, 2006). Part 3 includes an average of ten formative improvement strategies for each language function assessment.

Strategies to Enhance Speaking

Students can learn to be orally proficient in a language if certain basic strategies are met. The first is continuously speaking in the target language during class. The more the teachers speaks it under various situations, the more the students hear the language and feel comfortable in it according to the

FIGURE 1.4 Teacher Language Use in the Classroom

At the end of every minute, record a slash if you, the teacher, are speaking . . .	
Target Language	*English*
Total Target Language = _____ _____ ÷ (Total Target Language + Total English) = _____%	Total English = _____ _____ ÷ (Total Target Language + Total English) = _____%

"input" theory of Krashen (2003). In addition, students need to change from being only listeners of the target language to being speakers of it, according to Krashen's "output" theory. The teacher assesses their output. Language methodology has to move from students' hearing the language to speaking the language.

Three quick analyses can tell much about your language use in the class-room. The first is to audio record the class, listen to the recording, and then place a check mark every minute that you talk in English or the target language column (see Figure 1.4). For students to be immersed in the language in

FIGURE 1.5 Teacher and Student Language Use in the Classroom

At the end of every minute, record a slash if you, the teacher, or a student talks in the target language or English.		
	Target Language	*English*
Teacher	Total Teacher Talk in the Target Language = _____ or _____% of the sum of all four quadrants.	Total Teacher Talk in the English = _____ or _____% of the sum of all four quadrants.
Student	Total Student Talk in the Target Language = _____ or _____% of the sum of all four quadrants.	Total student Talk in the Modern Language = _____ or _____% of the sum of all four quadrants.

FIGURE 1.6 Students Speaking in the Target Language

At the end of every minute, record a slash to indicate how many times the students speak the target language.			
Word or phrase:	One sentence or full question:	Two to four consecutive sentences or questions:	Five or more consecutive sentences or questions:
Total = ____ or ____% of all four columns	Total = ____ or ____% of all four columns	Total = ____ or ____% of all four columns	Total = ____ or ____% of all four columns

class, they should hear the language at least 90% of class time from the beginning levels of language instruction (ACTFL, 2010). The second analysis is to study the recording again, this time looking for what percentage of time you or the students speak the target language (see Figure 1.5). At the end of every minute, record a slash in the Foreign Language-Teacher column if you have spoken in the target language and a slash in the Foreign Language-Student column if the students have spoken in that language. Students should be talking often in the class since they are the ones who need to become good speakers. A third analysis reveals the depth of the students' speaking (see Figure 1.6) when each student's utterance in the target language is recorded in the columns ranging from a short-word answer to a five-plus-consecutive sentence response.

Instead of recording information at the end of each minute, you may prefer to record the performance of each student. To do this, modify Figure 1.6 to include a listing of each student and record each time an individual student responds.

In addition to talking in the target language, a second strategy is to ensure that you are not teaching an overload of vocabulary for a topic. For example, students do not need to learn fifty items of clothing for their conversations. Verify that your vocabulary lists include the most common words that the students use in conversations. Students can filter your vocabulary lists by putting a check mark next to each word they find critical when talking about clothing. They may want certain words added. For example, although there may be five ways of saying "coat," they need just one. In a similar vein, make sure that they learn the everyday expressions for the topic of clothing, such as to "to buy," "to put on," "to wear," and "to take off."

A third strategy promotes student speaking when there are posters that display commonly used language statements and reactions. When students need a common expression, they can look at the appropriate poster. For example, there may be one poster that has agreeing/disagreeing statements such as "I agree," "I disagree," "I'm not sure," "What opinion do you have?" and "I agree . . . because . . . ."

A fourth strategy helps to develop your students' speaking abilities by having language use in the class be cumulative, not isolated. Integrate previous learning into the present learning. Occupation vocabulary and preference functions from a previous unit can be applied to the new unit's location vocabulary and explanation function. For example, students may make statements or ask questions like "What job does your father have?" "Where does he work?" "Does he like to work there?" and "Why?" Incorporate previous units of learning for the students since the textbooks do not usually do this. When students see a unit as "over," they often do not try to incorporate its concepts into their future learning. They easily forget the vocabulary, grammar, functions, and culture since they see no reason for remembering them.

A fifth strategy involves transforming each vocabulary and grammar learning into relevant communication for the student. When students realize that they can actually use this function, vocabulary, or grammar in a conversation with another person, they try harder to learn it. Ask the students how they would use these words in English in a conversation and then help them to transform those concepts into the target language. You may discover that the organizational pattern of the textbook bears little resemblance to how someone would actually speak about the topic. For example, a textbook may have main food dishes in one chapter, fruits and vegetables in the next, and preference words in a third chapter. For students to communicate about foods, they need the necessary vocabulary and grammar of a topic or situation presented at the same time so they can make meaningful statements.

The sixth strategy incorporates the use of speaking in homework. Instead of having students do ten written grammar exercises for homework, ask them to come to class with ten oral sentences or questions about the topic that involve the grammar point. For example, you can ask students to think of ten questions to ask another student about his or her daily routine. At the beginning of class, students ask the questions to their speaking partners and answer their speaking partners' questions. Students record the number of questions asked and answered and hand that sheet into you for you to monitor.

As a final oral strategy, you can implement formative assessment to change the culture of your classroom to be one that promotes constant student improvement and success. Once the students speak, you or other students can help them to improve. They learn you will give them new strategies to become better. Your class is not a "sink or swim" class; you are there to coach them to be great swimmers.

FIGURE 1.7 Monitoring and Class Time

Person doing the observation	Minute per student	Total students	Total minutes
1 (Teacher)	1	26	26
2 (Pairs)	1 for each of 2 students	26	2

Peer Formative Assessment

Rationale

Since you want your students to be speakers of the target language, you need to increase the students' opportunities to speak in class. But how can you assess all the students' speaking?

You are not the only one to monitor your students! Peers can also assess each other. As the following chart (Figure 1.7) demonstrates, if you (one person) listen for one minute to each of twenty-six students and record their speaking data, you take twenty-six minutes of class time. If you want to assess your students frequently such as twice a month, you will lose at least a class period a month or a total of more than ten class days (two weeks) during the year. Instead, have students in pairs listen to each other and record the speaking data. This monitoring will only take two minutes of class instead of the twenty-six that you would have to spend. This way, you will be able to monitor them more frequently. The benefits of peer assessment are that students become more engaged in the class, learn the assessment criteria more fully, learn to analyze speech more critically, and receive feedback more often in class. The previous oral homework assignment exemplifies this type of assessment. If, after the initial two minutes, you want students to give each other feedback for thirty seconds each, add another minute. Also, if you want the students to practice their feedback for half a minute each, then add another minute for a total of four minutes of class time Therefore, in only four minutes, students can speak and be assessed, be given feedback, and practice improvements based on that feedback.

Procedure

The criticisms of peer assessment, such as students "being nice due to peer pressure," "not knowing what to do," "being negative to each other," and "feeling the process is unfair," disappear when peer assessment is carefully implemented (Whitney, 2009). The following steps provide a procedure for introducing peer assessment to your students:

- First, explain to them that peer assessments are designed to help them become better in their target language. These formative assessments are not graded or marked; they exist solely for the students' growth.
- Secondly, tell them that a coach tells players what they do well but, more importantly, the coach shows them how to improve. If the players are not aware of what they are doing incorrectly and do not learn new strategies to become better, they continue with the same playing problems. Peer assessment serves as peer coaching. Fellow classmates will help their partners by telling them what they are doing well, what they are doing not so well, and how to improve.
- Thirdly, the peers should not use negative sentences such as "You did a horrible job." Instead, they should include objective factual statements and base their comments on the specific speaking goal and the criteria for this speaking task. Every statement leads to the students' overcoming a language problem. Model the type of formative feedback they should give such as, "You said four questions words; you did not use 'How' and 'Why.' Please make up questions using those words."
- Fourthly, explain to the students that you will gradually lead them through giving structured formative feedback to less structured feedback. Start them out with a simple counting of words or sentences that their partners say. Then they can move to listening and recording the presence of categories such as a home address or health. As they show success, proceed to less structured formative feedback that focuses on whole conversations or multiple assessments for the same speaking task.

Once you understand the how to implement a firm communication base in your class, the advantages of peer assessments, and the benefits of formative assessments, you can begin to apply formative assessment to your class speaking.

2

Formative Assessment Overview

Introduction

How can you help students become proficient speakers of their target language and climb up the ACTFL proficiency levels? When students demonstrate speaking problems in the target language and do not receive new strategies for improvement, they dig themselves into a hole. As they develop more problems, this hole grows bigger and bigger until it becomes a canyon. Instead of improving, they become trapped by all their previous speaking problems. In the formative assessment process, the focus is on student improvement: the teacher assesses the present status of the students and immediately provides the students with specific strategies so they can begin to improve. This process incorporates monitoring, diagnosing, and providing feedback for students' continual success.

Imagine your car makes a horrible, loud noise and you do not know what is wrong. You take it to a mechanic. The mechanic listens to the car, looks under the hood, and takes it on a test drive. If he says, "You've got a serious problem. Leave!" you would be very upset. You would want to know what is wrong and how it can be fixed. Unfortunately, this scenario is a metaphor of what happens in many language classrooms. Students receive grades or comments on their speaking that do not help them understand specifically what they can do to improve. Most of the traditional foreign language speaking comments, such as "Practice more," do not tell the students how to improve. If the students encounter more speaking problems, soon their "speaking car" does not run. They want their mechanic (you) to help them become better speakers.

The formative assessment approach, which is relatively new to foreign language education, shares similarities with the earlier strategy-based learning. Both formative assessment and strategy-based learning focus on students' continual improvement through providing specific strategies that lead directly to positive change. In strategy-based learning, the teacher directly gives students cognitive, metacognitive, social, and affective strategies to use before, during, and after a conversation (Chamot, 2004). For example, one metacognitive strategy for students is to plan out their conversation by thinking through its key points before they begin to speak. Each strategy provides a specific way in which the students improve their speaking skills. The teacher checks to see if the students use these strategies and has them evaluate themselves on their use of these strategies.

Formative assessment is the process of assessing students' present learning and then providing them with specific strategies that directly lead to their "immediate" improvement (Heritage, 2007; Tuttle, 2009). This continual growth cycle includes monitoring the students' speaking, diagnosing the students' strengths and weaknesses, supplying the students with new or paraphrased strategies, and allowing the students to use that feedback to improve.

When teachers use formative assessment, students can learn in six to seven months what would normally take a school year to learn (Leahy, Lyon, Thompson, & Wiliam, 2005). Furthermore, Ainsworth and Viegut (2006, p. 23) explain that when you use formative assessment, you are better able to: determine what standards students already know and to what degree; decide what changes to make in instruction so that all students succeed; create appropriate lessons, activities, and groupings; and inform students about their progress in order to help them set goals. In addition, the research of Black and Wiliam (1998) emphasizes that this approach works extremely well with at-risk students.

Formative assessment can be compared to a doctor's visit. At the doctor's office, a nurse takes your vital signs (monitors you). The doctor asks you some additional questions or examines you (monitors you). Then the doctor compares your present condition to a healthy condition in order to determine your medical condition (diagnosis for achievement). Afterwards, he decides what strategy will help you improve (diagnosis for strategy). Next, this doctor informs you of your condition and the strategy for improvement in such a way that you will understand your condition and will want to use that strategy (feedback). You take the medicine for the designated time (the specific feedback strategy for improvement) so that your body can improve (time for growth). In the end, you feel healthy again (reporting growth). Figure 2.1 shows the formative assessment process applied to speaking.

Just as the doctor's office visit is a seamless process, the formative assessment process for speaking in the language classroom becomes a natural part of the classroom. By modifying what you already do, you can implement the formative assessment process for improved student speaking. You can consider yourself the students' personal classroom navigation device (or GPS) that continually redirects students toward the speaking goal destination when they get off the learning path.

FIGURE 2.1 Formative Assessment and Speaking

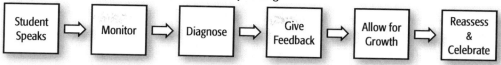

Formative assessment should be implemented early in the language course so students can become proficient speakers. Students' early speaking habits are like cement that quickly hardens unless you can modify these habits very early in the process (Hunter, 1976). Therefore, formative assessment should begin as soon as the students think about their first speaking task, not after they have waited to have a speaking test at the ten-week mark or at the end of the year. Likewise, formative assessment focuses on the students overcoming their most critical speaking learning gaps first and then working down to the less critical ones. This way, students can make giant improvement steps in their oral communication.

You can build formative assessment into the classroom on a regularly occurring basis to guarantee success at each step of the speaking process. By taking a major speaking task and breaking it down into its parts, you can assess and give feedback on each critical part using assessments that last just a few minutes. For example, for the speaking prompt of eating in a restaurant, students have to be familiar with speaking tasks such as greetings, identifying foods, asking about foods, stating preferences, requesting food, expressing any problems, and asking for the bill. As students become proficient at these small speaking tasks, they experience small language wins. Their small wins accumulate into a big win: they increase their confidence as speakers in the target language. The students know that if they show a speaking gap, they will instantly be given formative feedback to improve their speaking. They are no longer crawling in their language use; rather, they are walking and running in their speaking.

Formative assessment plays a key role in Response to Intervention (RTI), in which you instruct, monitor, diagnose, and give feedback so students can improve on essential skills (Howell, Patton, & Deiotte, 2008). In RTI Tier 1, the universal- or classroom level-intervention is sufficient for 80% of students. Here, you should look for red flags that show a lack of achievement (monitor the students), intervene with a new strategy or a modification of an existing strategy (diagnose and give feedback), and reassess students. If students do not show growth after numerous tries, another strategy or modification can be used. If the students still do not show progress, they move to Tier 2 (Small Group Intervention) and, if necessary, to Tier 3 (Personalized, Intensive Instruction). Usually, 15% of students move to Tier 2 and 5% move to Tier 3. The formative assessment idea of helping students succeed at critical skills is crucial to RTI, as is the idea that students need immediate intervention to be able to grow.

Formative assessment implies ongoing, continuous assessment and feedback. Teachers provide assessments so students can see their growth over time. For example, in the first assessment of the socializing function, students may only be able to say two greeting statements to a stranger. As the year goes on and the students learn more information, their numbers of socializing statements increase to where they can have full conversations on a wide range of topics.

An additional benefit of formative assessment is that it saves you time in class. Since the assessments and feedback take so little time (about four minutes), you can easily administer an assessment each class. Since the assessments help students improve, you do not have to spend time going over and over the same mistakes. Additionally, as students become successful at the various speaking assessments, they can use their speaking strategies to help them in their listening, reading, and writing in the target language. For example, students who use the questions word strategy to ask questions become better equipped to answer question words found in a reading passage. Also, formative assessments energize the class since all students are actively engaged in talking or listening for a minute or more. The students become excited by being able to talk about a topic at length in their target language.

Pre-Formative Assessment

Before you begin the steps of formative assessment, you need to establish some basic groundwork. The formative assessment process includes *informing the learners of the speaking learning goal and of the high level of speaking performance expected* based on the 1999 ACTFL Proficiency Guidelines (Figure 2.2). Language learning becomes demystified through the sharing of learning goals and success criteria (Black & Jones, 2006). When students understand what they are to learn and how they will be assessed, they begin to move forward in their learning. Share the learning goal in student talk, not in academic jargon. Students at the Advanced level of the ACTFL proficiency guide speak in complex sentences using different tenses rather than the "Novice" level in which the students respond in simple memorized sentences in the present tense. Let the students know what the specific critical assessment areas are for each learning activity. For example, you may ask them to say five complex sentences using "because" to tell their preference for which movie to go see. Before administering the assessment, share with them what vocabulary, grammar, and cultural information they will need to be successful in this language activity. Model the type of speaking to be used by showing them a video or having them listen to a sample conversation about a similar

FIGURE 2.2 High Level of Performance for the Speaking Goal

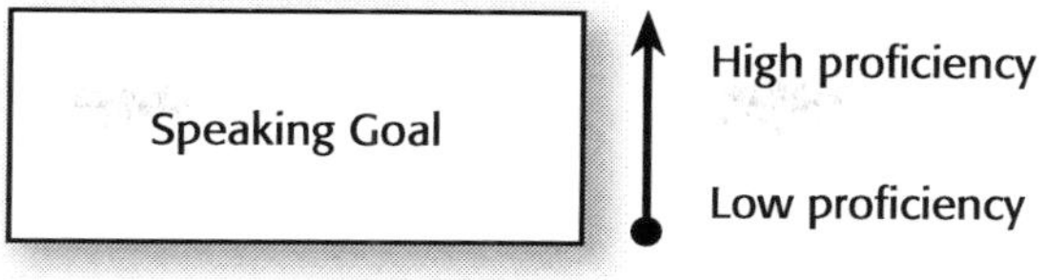

topic. You can also have students evaluate a recorded conversation by using the speaking checklist so they can come to realize the various levels of proficiency in a conversation.

Next, decide on the formative assessment that you will use for this particular speaking goal and on the format of this formative assessment. Will you use a standards-based rubric, a checklist, or a counting tool to monitor the students? How will you make sure that the assessment measures critical components of the task? How will you incorporate a new strategy to move the students forward? Decide if you will use the same assessment tool each time or a variation on the assessment. If you use the same assessment tool each time, they can compare results over time. If you only use variations, then you will be unable to compare the results against each other.

The final pre-formative assessment step includes a *preassessment* of the students' present speaking skills. Find out the background experiences that students have with the given speaking goal. For example, for a restaurant speaking topic, ask them at the beginning of the unit to express their likes and dislikes for ten foods. You can also have them complete a written self-assessment of their ability to perform a series of specific restaurant-related speaking tasks (Figure 2.3). If you want, you can quickly verify the students' written self-assessment by asking them to perform the indicated speaking tasks. From these short preassessments, you can begin to determine their backgrounds in this speaking goal and adjust your instruction accordingly.

FIGURE 2.3 Written Self-Assessment Preassessment

Tenses

I can (put a plus sign [+] if you can do it):

___ Name at least ten foods.
___ Tell at least five food descriptions, such as spicy and cold.
___ Tell what I like about two different foods.
___ Explain a common restaurant problem and how to solve it.

Monitor

Until your students speak in the target language, you cannot help them improve. Once they speak, you can begin the formative assessment process. The more often they talk in class, the more opportunities you have to help them overcome their speaking gaps and move up the proficiency levels. Likewise, when you give them speaking tasks that focus on a particular speaking skill, such as expressing likes or dislikes for gifts or describing something, you can observe oral proficiency specifics as opposed to observing general oral proficiency.

In the formative assessment monitoring stage (Figure 2.4), you, the students' peers, a language speaker, or the students frequently observe and collect data on the specific speaking task. This monitoring involves collecting real-time data from the students to identify their level of speaking at the present moment. Data from six months ago or even from two weeks ago is outdated. Monitoring present data only includes observation and collection of the speaking results; the analysis of the data takes place in the Diagnosis stage.

Formative assessment monitoring becomes embedded in the classroom through assessments of student speaking that occur daily, multiple times a week, or weekly. These assessments focus on normal classroom speaking activities, not on special speaking tests. Your in-class speaking assessments take little time; the student speaks and an observer simultaneously collects the information on the speaking. Here's an example:

> Taylor, a sixth-grade Spanish student, speaks for a minute and a half about various alternatives to a class scheduling problem and the advantages of each alternative. At the same time, her peer observer, Kadir, makes a mark for each alternative and its advantages. Then, Kadir talks about a problem with his class schedule and its various alternative solutions while Taylor does the recording.

The whole monitoring of speaking takes three minutes of class time! As you include other components of formative assessment, the time will increase slightly.

FIGURE 2.4 Monitoring Phase of Formative Assessment

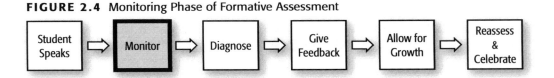

When you base your classroom speaking activities on a specific aspect of the ACTFL Speaking Proficiency Guidelines, you have built in valid assessments. Monitor specific aspects, such as the students' ability to "exchange greetings" in the Novice-Low level or their ability to express "immediate need" (e.g. ordering food) in the Intermediate-Low level. Observe for specific proficiency, not for the ambiguous "being a good speaker" or "doing a great job."

As noted in Part 1, peers can assess each other to maximize the time that students are monitored.

A Few Ways to Monitor Students' Speaking

- ◆ Count elements of the students' speech, such as how many sentences they say, questions they answer, task-related vocabulary, contrast words, and future tense verbs (see Figure 2.5).
- ◆ Use checklists for language use, such as which question words the students ask, task related vocabulary they use, functions they employ, or aspects of the topic they speak about. Checklists cover areas from simple vocabulary to more general speaking skills, such as the students' ability to tell a story (monologue) about an event. One form of a checklist is "I-can" statements that identify what the student can do by the end of the unit, such as the Family Unit for beginning levels in Figure 2.6 on page 24 (Dann, 2009; Fall, Adair-Hauck, & Gilsan, 2007). In a more advanced form of self-reflection (Figure 2.7, page 24), students identify what they can do to improve.
- ◆ Utilize classroom seating charts (Figure 2.8, page 25) to identify the type of target language response the students make and the

FIGURE 2.5 Count Monitoring By Using a Chart

	Student 1	Student 2
Conversation: Each time your partner asks a critical question about the topic, make a slash (/) under his or her name. At the end of the time limit, record the total number of slashes in that category. For example, for Student 1 in "Critical Questions," /// = 3.		
Critical Questions		

FIGURE 2.6 Monitoring Through a Checklist of I-Can Statements

---

Topic: Family

I can (put a plus sign [+] if you can do it):

___ Name 10 family members.
___ Give the names and ages of the family members and state their relationship to me.
___ Describe three of them with at least four descriptive words each.
___ Describe three family members' likes/dislikes and favorite activities.
___ Tell something another family member and I like to do together.
___ Retell a conversation in which I disagreed with another family member.

---

frequency of their responses. For example, as you do your daily class warm-up by questioning individual students or as you ask individual students questions during class, you can use symbols to record if the student does not respond (0), responds with a few words (F), responds with a sentence (S), responds with a complex answer (C), or responds and asks a probing question about the topic (?). Your symbols provide rich information for future diagnosis.

♦ Listen in on individual, pair, or group work. As students do oral work in pairs or small groups, walk around the room to monitor their speaking. For example, have your students sit in small groups

FIGURE 2.7 Student's Self-Assessment of Some Language Functions and Topics

Place a plus sign (+) under each function that you can do for the topic of clothing. Be prepared to give an example.

Functions	Give information	State preferences	Ask for opinions	Agree/ Disagree	Explain
Topic: Clothing					

I am good at: _____

_____

I can become better in the areas of: _____

_____

What I will do to be better in these areas: _____

_____

FIGURE 2.8 Monitoring Class Warm-Ups with a Seating Chart

Flores, Tina 0 F F 0 0	Velez, Maria S C S C ?	Olsen, Butch F F F F	Smith, Jack ? C ? ? C	Hanson, James S S F S F
Yacob, Roz 0 0 0 F 0	Lee, Kim F F S F S	Zang, Merin C C C C ?	Santiago, Daritza ? ? ? C ?	Holberg, Keziah S S C S S

and speak in round-robin manner (go around the circle with each student giving an answer) to explain whether or not the basketball team will win this weekend and why. Observe and record how well they state their opinions and their reasoning.

Record Keeping

As you, another adult, or another student monitors the students, record the speaking information (number and type of sentences spoken) to have it available for diagnosis. You can keep a paper record, such as a 3x5 card for each learning goal, a separate sheet with all the major components of the learning goal and a series of mail labels for each major language function. However, if you use a spreadsheet, you will make future analysis much easier.

Diagnose

After the specific speaking goal has been identified and students' speaking has been monitored by collecting sufficient real-time information, the diagnosis phase begins (Figure 2.9). A pattern is indicated when a student demonstrates the same learning gap over multiple assessments.

The diagnosis process consists of two distinct parts (Figure 2.10, page 26). In the first part, the teacher compares the present status of the students to the expected level in the speaking proficiency and then identifies their precise strength(s) and learning gap(s) in specific student-friendly terms. For example:

FIGURE 2.9 Diagnosing Phase of Formative Assessment

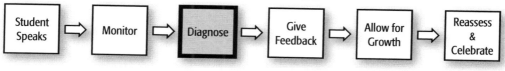

FIGURE 2.10 Two Parts of Diagnosis

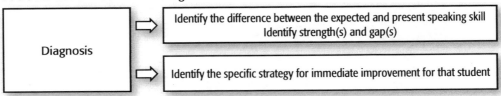

Jordan role plays being the parent of a teenager who has not come home until 2:00 am on a school night while another student plays the teenager. The teacher (or another observer) identifies that Jordan has fulfilled the requirement of asking five different questions and, therefore, has a strength in asking family-related questions. The observer also identifies that Jordan does not vary the strength of the questions when the teenager does not give much information about why he is late.

In the second part of diagnosis, the teacher identifies a specific strategy or strategies that will directly and immediately help Jordan overcome this function learning gap. For example, in one specific strategy, you can plan to show her a teacher-made sheet she has in her notebook that lists request functions that range from polite to demanding and show her which phrases she might use to be more forceful in her communications.

The improvement strategy has to be a specific one that includes concrete actions. A strategy cannot be vague or nebulous, such as "Work harder," "Focus," "Practice more," "Talk more," or "Think about it." These phrases do not provide specific improvement strategies; the students still have no idea of what to do to improve.

Usually, the process of going from monitoring to diagnosis happens in a flash. The observer goes directly from monitoring to the two parts of diagnosis. Similarly, the process of diagnosis can usually be done in a flash: the student's learning gap is _____ and the student can use the strategy of _____ to improve in speaking.

By building up a library of potential speaking gaps and the specific strategies to overcome them, you can find an appropriate strategy more easily. You can create a paper library, such as a journal or a Word document. If you create a speaking gaps wiki (an online collaboration tool) using, for instance, PBworks (pbworks.com), you can invite other teachers of your target language to work with you so that you all collectively build the library. By using a wiki, you can learn from the new strategies presented by your colleagues. All of you will have many strategies for any learning gap so that you can select the best one for a particular student. The students will also benefit if you can give them a list of various strategies, such as those strategies listed in Part 3.

Some students will show that their proficiency during the first diagnosis of an assessment. These students can set their own improvement goals, such as saying ten percent more the next time or increasing their vocabulary beyond the basic vocabulary. Formative assessment focuses on constant improvement for all students, even those who show proficiency in the first assessment.

The diagnosis phase stops with these two parts; you give the diagnostic information to the student in the Feedback Phase of formative assessment.

Give Feedback

Once you have monitored the students' oral skills, diagnosed their present abilities relative to the learning goal, and identified an appropriate strategy that will directly move them forward in their oral skills, you are ready to give the students formative feedback so they can improve (Figure 2.11). Formative feedback can be given in the language the students more easily understand; beginning students should be given feedback in English while advanced students can be given feedback in the target language.

Formative feedback focuses on how and what is said to the students so that they will 1) understand what you said, 2) emotionally accept what is being said, 3) be willing to make a change, and 4) actually implement the change (Figure 2.12, page 28). Bender (2007) stresses that any person giving feedback needs to have an encouraging coaching attitude.

Hattie (1998) states that formative feedback is "the most powerful single moderator in the enhancement of achievement." Feedback serves the purpose of preventing your students from repeating the same errors and, therefore, making those errors part of the students' mental strategies (Willis, 2006). Feedback is formative if it leads to improved student learning (Wiggins, 1998; Black & Wiliam, 1999). Tomlinson and McTighe (2006, p. 78) verify that feedback is formative by asking, "Can the learners tell specifically from the given feedback what they have done well and what they could do next time to improve? If not, the feedback is not specific or understandable enough for the learner."

Students are more likely to accept feedback when they understand the specific speaking proficiency that they are to reach and the high quality of

FIGURE 2.11 Feedback Phase of Formative Assessment

Student Speaks ⇨ Monitor ⇨ Diagnose ⇨ Give Feedback ⇨ Allow for Growth ⇨ Reassess & Celebrate

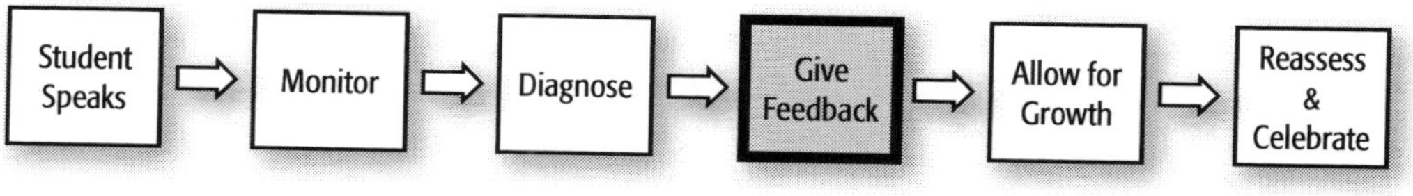

FIGURE 2.12 Formative Feedback to Change

speaking expected of them. When students are clear about the learning goal and they know that their teacher and their classmates are helping them to achieve it, they feel more motivated to improve (McTighe & O'Connor, 2006).

Feedback Characteristics

All feedback generally has the same characteristics (Black and Wiliam, 1998; Stiggins, 2007; Heritage, 2007; Tuttle, 2009; Moss & Brookhart, 2009). The teacher or peer:

- ♦ Bases feedback on the standard learning goal specific such as "You have shown that you can talk about a past event"; avoids non-goal statements about behavior, attitude, attire, neatness, or PowerPoint skill; and avoids comparing the student to other students with statements such as "The rest of the class understands this."
- ♦ Focuses on only two to three critical feedback points at a time (students can usually accept three criticisms but they may emotionally "shut down" if they hear more) and avoids the tendency of correcting everything the students say.
- ♦ Provides concrete suggestions for improvement and avoids vague, ineffective general instructional terms like "Work harder" and "Be more thoughtful."
- ♦ Succinctly and directly communicates the strength or the gap to the students (e.g., "You know the vocabulary for clothing. You can improve by learning how to ask clothing-related questions such as those asked in a clothing store").
- ♦ Suggests a small, manageable change rather than a large, complex one that the students cannot envision. Students learn to tell what they like before they learn to give reasons to explain their preferences.
- ♦ Is immediate or timely and gives the feedback as soon after the performance task as possible—the longer the delay, the less meaningful the feedback.
- ♦ Gives constant feedback. You or peers give feedback on a daily or weekly basis so students can improve on a daily or weekly basis.

- Allows for students' own feedback. Students are encouraged to constantly self-assess and change strategies to transform learning gaps into learning strengths.
- Asks for students' commitment to change and helps the students move from knowing about the need for change to wanting to make the improvement changes.

Feedback can be divided into some general categories (Primary Source, 2004; Lipton and Wellman, 1999; Jefferson Parish Public Schools, n.d.; Brookhart, 2009). To do this, you:

- Accept the students' difficulty in the learning and share that you want to help them. Example: "I know you are struggling with this. I'm here to help you."
- Focus the students on the learning purpose with statements. Example: "Let's re-examine what you are to do for this speaking task."
- Remind students of the high quality of the standards-based learning expected of them through rubrics, numeric scales, and exemplars. Example: "What do you have to do to do well in this speaking situation?"
- Paraphrase students' responses to help them clarify their thinking about their speaking with statements. Example: "You said that you liked the movie. What examples can you give to explain why you like the movie?"
- Scaffold the students' learning as they start or during their work. Example: "Let's break this speaking task down by . . . ."
- You deliver these statements or questions in a caring and nurturing tone or at least a neutral tone instead of a judgmental or criticizing tone.

Feedback in your target language classroom can have several formats. Based on the number of students in the class with the same learning gap, the new strategy can be delivered to the whole class, half the class, a small group, or an individual. Go from a broad brush stroke (for helping the greatest number of students at the same time with the identical learning gap) to finer brush strokes (for the gap that only half the class displays) to tiny brushes (for a gap limited to a small group or an individual). Give your feedback orally (speak some quick comments), in writing (use a checklist with comments), with a gesture (move your hand over your shoulder to indicate when a past-tense verb should be used), or with technology (give a PowerPoint explanation on relevant speaking tasks).

Some Formative Feedback Techniques

Help Sheet

For each learning goal, prepare a sheet that has the essential nouns, verbs, adjectives, grammatical structures, cultural information, common questions, and reaction phrases listed in separate columns. Once you, the students' partners, or the students have individually identified a learning gap, the students look at the learning goal help sheet for assistance. For example, if the students cannot think of reaction words, the students look at the reaction phrases column and practice those reactions until they can incorporate them into the conversation.

Technology

Most students react positively to technology-based feedback. You or your students who have already met the learning goal can find or produce PowerPoints, YouTube movies, podcasts, or other media forms that can provide alternative strategies to learning the given concept. For example, in order to learn about the language function of giving information, students can watch a student-made mini-iMovie in which a student who has just moved into a neighborhood asks a person from the neighborhood what there is to do.

Mini-Focus

At the beginning of a class, inform the students of what particular speaking criteria you are going to assess, such as the use of conversation fillers like "um" in English. After a quick peer assessment and a look at the recorded results, go over their most common strengths and the most common areas that need improvement. Then ask the class to suggest some strategies for improvement. You may also propose some. The students practice those new strategies immediately.

Speed Dating Service

For this feedback technique, half the pupils (the sitters) remain at their desks to ask questions; the other half (the movers) rotate round the room, visiting the sitters one at a time. The sitters ask the movers questions about a given topic, such as *work*. The movers answer the questions for one minute. After the movers finish talking, the sitters use Figure 2.13 to write down feedback about their strengths and an area for specific improvement based on the specific skill you have identified, and return the sheet to the movers. The movers look at the area for growth, think about how they will improve, and practice that improvement. After a minute of feedback and practice, signal the movers to go to their new "dates" to talk about the same topic. The same process is repeated at least three times so the movers have four opportunities to improve. Then students switch roles; the previous sitters become the movers (Salt, 2010).

FIGURE 2.13 Reviewers Positives and Area for Improvement (Partial)

Name: _____ Task: _____ Date: _____

Reviewer: After you listen to the speaker, write two specific good things your partner did, such as answering all the questions, next to the plus signs (+). Then write one very specific way in which he/she can improve next to the arrow (→).

Reviewer 1

+ _____

+ _____

→ _____

Reviewer 2

+ _____

+ _____

→ _____

Examine a Speaking Exemplar

In this technique, students speak on a topic, listen to a digital exemplar, such as a teacher-made iMovie, compare the exemplar to their own speaking, and then revise their speaking. As they listen to the exemplar, they should listen to how the digital speaker completes the task, rather than the exact words used by the speaker. For example, students might listen to someone expressing his preferences for sports when they are assigned to express their preferences for clothing. Students write out the similarities and differences between the exemplar and their own speaking. Alternatively, they might use a teacher-provided checklist that suggests strategies to improve, such as using preference words. Students decide how they can improve and take the time to practice; then they speak again on the same topic.

The Weekly Class Speaking Average and Strategies

By using technology, you can show the class its progress and, more importantly, provide feedback on how to improve. To monitor the students' speaking fluency, give the students a prompt, such as "Tell me about a problem at a party." They speak for a minute and a half and their partners record the sentences said. Then they record the number of sentences in their sentence log along with the date (Figure 2.14, page 32). Give the students another activity, lasting about five minutes. During the activity, go around the room, take students' scores, and record them in the speaking fluency spreadsheet,

FIGURE 2.14 Sentence Log

Class:

Amount of sentences said in 1.5 minutes on the topic of _____ and the function of elaboration.

Date								
Number								

Strategies suggested by other class members:

A strategy I will try:

kept on a computer, PDA, tablet computer, or mobile device. Use a computer to calculate and graph the class average for that week.

Project the spreadsheet image to show the students the average class total for that week, without showing any individual score (Figure 2.15), and identify whether the class has increased from the last week. Although this assessment does not focus on the individual, each individual automatically compares the class average with his or her own. By asking students who scored

FIGURE 2.15 Class Average Increase in Speaking

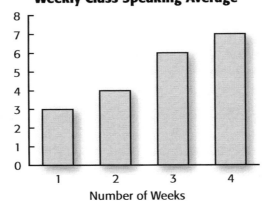

Weekly Class Speaking Average

Number of Weeks

above the class average to share what strategies they used, everyone in the classroom learns new strategies to become better speakers. Then the students select a new strategy they want to try and practice this strategy. Post the class average graph for each week of assessment in the classroom and encourage students to try to beat their previous score and/or the class average.

Provide Another Strategy

If your students try out their new strategy numerous times and they do not advance in the proficiency, share a different strategy with them. Suggest strategies that will be effective for the students.

Allow for Growth

When your students have been monitored, diagnosed for their learning strengths or gaps, offered a strategy, and given their feedback in a friendly and inviting manner, they are ready to overcome their speaking learning gaps. When students have time immediately after receiving formative feedback to practice and improve, they make tremendous gains (Figure 2.16). The more they delay their practice and potential improvement, the less likely they are to succeed. Medicine has the "golden hour" concept of immediacy; the greatest chance for the survival of a person with multi-system trauma occurs within the first sixty minutes after the trauma. Our students' "golden hour" is the time immediately after receiving the feedback and it lasts less than fifteen minutes. Once they leave the language classroom, their likelihood of improving decreases dramatically.

Build in class time immediately after each formative feedback to allow the students to grow in their oral proficiency until they reach the proficiency level you have predetermined. This short "time for growth," two to five minutes of classroom time, reaps enormous dividends as your struggling speakers overcome their speaking gaps. Activities done during their "golden hour" of treatment helps them to move forward to be healthy learners. Depending on the number of learners who have the same speaking learning gap, you probably will have several small groups, each with different major learning

FIGURE 2.16 Growth Phase of Formative Assessment

| Student Speaks | ⇨ | Monitor | ⇨ | Diagnose | ⇨ | Give Feedback | ⇨ | Allow for Growth | ⇨ | Reassess & Celebrate |

FIGURE 2.17 Class Speaking Gap Groups and Activities Immediately After Feedback

Student Grouping	Ten students who are proficient	Seven students with the same "grammar structure" learning gap	Five students with the same "talking about a picture" learning gap	Two students with the same "connecting sentences" learning gap	One student with a "how to answer questions" learning gap
Targeted Formative Practice	Students work in pairs to write out various conversations as samples for other students. They may illustrate their conversations to help others better comprehend how to overcome learning gaps.	Students individually read over a teacher-made handout and then use teacher-provided flashcards to practice the grammar structure. They check their answers by looking at the back of the cards.	Students listen to a digitized speech found on the class wiki to hear three speakers identify the different strategies they use. Then the students individually select a strategy and talk about a picture using the new strategy.	Students do a workbook page in which there is a list of connectors to put into a conversation. They check their answers against an answer key that has an explanation for each answer.	The student meets with you on how to answer questions.

gaps (Figure 2.17). Small groups provide differentiation for your students. Successful small groups use very targeted materials that lead directly to their improvement. Furthermore, the groups work independently of you so you can spend more time with a specific group or with an individual.

Reassess and Celebrate

Students, parents, administrators, and you want to see the students grow in their speaking abilities (Figure 2.18). You can report their advancement in many ways. Have students keep their own logs of their progress in specific speaking skills, such as a log of when they go beyond speaking in the present tense to using the past and future tenses. They can record their success using "I can" or skill statements as they are able to perform more speaking tasks. You can also keep classroom charts of the class' advances in certain oral proficiency skills over time, such as their skill in asking and answering questions over a two month period. Parents can log into the class website or wiki to see the progress of the class and, on a secure website, to see individual speaking grades and class averages on specific speaking proficiencies. Once you create a list of the oral skills that all students in your class can perform, you can post it on the class website or wiki and send it to parents or administrators. You may also create an award certificate for achieving a major language skill, such as being able to tell a story about a personal event. Lastly, you can show your students a graph of what percentage of students have become proficient at skills at the Intermediate Level. As you add information to the graph, you and others can measure advancement over time in your class.

All of the previous growth areas can be cause for celebration. Specifically, whenever students successfully demonstrate growth in a major component of their speaking, such as give and take directions to a given location, you can help them celebrate their success by doing such things as applauding them, shaking their hands, or drawing a smiley face on their paper assignments. Likewise, if students complete several major components, such as giving information, asking questions, sharing opinions, and disagreeing about a topic, you can award them a certificate of communication for that language function. Reward speaking that demonstrates the learning goal. Students can draw huge check marks on their learning goal sheet as they complete

FIGURE 2.18 Reassessing and Celebrating Phase of Formative Assessment

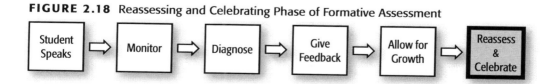

each sub-part of the learning goal and they can draw stars on the bottom of the sheet when they successfully complete the whole goal. Other celebration ideas include posting students' names on a "Speaking Fame Wall" as they show their proficiency in a speaking area and sponsoring an after-school "tea" where students can demonstrate their skills to their parents. In this way, your class changes from a place of undiscovered successes to a constant celebration of learning successes.

One way to showcase student growth is through student portfolios in which students include their own examples to show that they have achieved learning goals. Your students can create their own portfolios using Power-Point, a wiki, or a multimedia program. Linguafolio, from the University of Oregon, exemplifies a portfolio which includes: a mode, such as Speaking; a level, such as Novice-Mid; an "I can" statement, such as "I can say words on a familiar topic"; a topic, such as "food"; a function, such as "List"; a prompt or visual, such as a sign for a restaurant; and the student's evidence that he/she has achieved this level (Bivens, n.d.).

Grading

How do you grade your students' speaking in a formative assessment environment (Wiggins, 1998)? The score on any formative assessment should not be entered in your grade book as a traditional summative test might be; formative assessments are for student improvement, not for grades. How do you move from summative to formative grading?

Comments Are Better than a Grade

If you give students a grade on their speaking and also include written comments for improvements, they will not look at the written feedback (Butler, 1988). The grade literally cancels out any comments. It is better to only give comments, without a grade. An alternative strategy is to give a grade after the students reach the desired proficiency level, such as being able to ask six different important questions about a given topic.

Proficient Grades

If your students, their parents, or administration insist on an oral proficiency grade, you still have many options. One option consists of indicating at what ACTFL proficiency level the students are, such as the Intermediate-Low level. Another option includes using a list of "I-can" statements or a list of the major skills in each proficiency level; you or your student can put a plus sign (+) in front of each statement that the student can demonstrate. In an alternative option, you count the number of "I-can" statements or number of major skills in each proficiency level that a student has demonstrated, divide that number by the total number of "I-can" statements, and give that percent as a grade.

When you use a scoring system for speaking assessments, you can analyze your students' speaking at a micro level. For example, the Intermediate level consists of many different language proficiencies. If you record micro scores (e.g., 60, 65, 74, and 80) on each assessment within that level (e.g., progress in using the "agree and disagree" functions), then you can see the students' progress over time in each individual task. Likewise, since you have these scores on a computer spreadsheet, you can sort students' scores from low to high to see which students have demonstrated proficiency and which ones need additional help before they become proficient.

Improved Grades

In a formative assessment mentality, you want students to reach a proficient or high level of speaking, and that achievement should be fully rewarded. In a formative assessment system, a student who scores a 63, a 73, and then a 90 on an assessment should receive a 90 since he/she has reached the proficient level. In most real life tasks, you either succeed or you do not. No matter how many times people take a drivers' test and fail it, they can still pass it. Imagine if future drivers' "failing scores" were averaged in with their "passing scores"; most would never get their license.

As a variation, you can give a slightly different score for improvement on assessments. Score all initial grades as even numbers: 92 for above proficient, 86 for proficient, 76 for improving, and 66 for developing. Then score improved performances with the next higher odd number. For example, if a student with an initial score of 77 demonstrates improved proficiency, you can give him an 85, a score one point lower than the proficient score. Then you will be able to look at your grade book to determine which students received an original score of 86 and which earned an improved score of 85 on a certain speaking task. The one point difference between 86 and 85 has a very minimal impact on the final grade, yet it allows you to analyze students' improvements.

Cumulative Grading

Unfortunately, averaging students' speaking scores or weighting the last score still does not acknowledge that students have reached a level of proficiency.

For example, if a student completes four speaking tasks during the year involving the same speaking function and receives scores of 70, 75, 80, and 85, his average is 77.5. Not only is this average score below two of the highest grades, but the averaged score does not represent the student's highest achievement.

A truly formative approach to grading is to award the students their highest speaking grades (often their final grades) as their summative grades for speaking. They have reached that level, so they deserve the higher grade. The real question for you is how you reward students' growth in speaking over time.

Summative Grading of Speaking

After students have done a series of formative speaking assessments on the same language function over time, received feedback, and practiced the improvement strategy, then they can take a summative speaking test on that function. The students should know the teacher's goal for their speaking. For example, if a teacher decides that she wants students to be able to ask and answer five questions about a topic (five questions and five answers, ten sentences total) in a minute, she transforms these numbers into a summative grading system: 9-10 sentences = A, 8 sentences = B, 7 sentences = C.

Transform Classroom Activities into Formative Activities

You can transform many classroom activities into oral proficiency formative assessments. Blaz (2001) provides a comprehensive list of different ways to speak in the classroom.

answer prompt cards	PowerPoint presentation
debate	react to a visual/TV/Movie
demonstration/How-to speech	react to music/speech
description	retell a story/TV show
dialogue	review of TV/Movie
documentary	role playing
group problem solving	sell something
interview	simulation
monologue	skit
narration	speech
newscast/weather report	speech in favor or against
podcast	song or rap

FIGURE 2.19 Peer-Assessment of TV Show Reaction

Does the partner (Answer with Y [Yes] or NY[Not Yet]):

___ Respond appropriately to my questions and statements. (For example, if I ask, "Where are the people?" he/she responds with a place.)

___ Use accurate language? (For example, he/she uses the past tense to tell about actions happening in the past. He/she has the noun and verb agree such as "He sings.")

___ Use vocabulary well? (For example, he/she uses precise vocabulary, such as "the shirt" instead of the more general "clothing." He/she uses a wide variety of words.)

___ Use cultural knowledge about the topic? (For example, he/she mentions when meal time is in the language country.)

___ Maintain the conversation? (For example, he/she asks me questions as well as answering my questions. He/She elaborates on something I said.)

My partner's area(s) of strength:

An area that he/she can develop:

What he/she can do to develop this area:

You can take these normal classroom activities and turn them into formative ones by deciding 1) what the specific speaking goal is, 2) what its critical parts or functions are, 3) what assessment will be used to evaluate the speaking, and 4) what strategies will help the students be successful in overcoming language gaps. For example, you may create a peer-review checklist based on the ACTFL Guidelines for talking about a reaction to a TV show (Figure 2.19).

Now that you understand the basics of formative assessment, you can move on to actually using speaking formative assessments in your classroom. Part 3 of this book assesses seventeen different language functions.

3

Speaking Formative Assessments

Overview

The following interpersonal speaking assessments generally increase in difficulty, starting at the lower levels of the ACTFL Guidelines. You can select which ones to use and the order in which to use them according to your curriculum. You may choose to use these in a wide variety of ways, such as warm-ups, transition activities, motivators, after some initial practice of a learning goal, or end-of-the-class activities. The assessments have three basic parts: your instructions for the assessment, the students' assessment form, and the students' formative strategies. Each activity takes about three minutes to get the student baseline speaking score and to do quick peer feedback. When each of the students practices using the feedback, the total time increases by just one minute to a total of four minutes. These few minutes change your class into one that allows your students to become speakers of the target language.

Each assessment uses the following structure:

♦ Purpose
♦ ACTFL Proficiency Level and Speaking Type
♦ Student Grouping
♦ Assessment Form
♦ Full Procedure
♦ Implementing Formative Feedback
♦ Extension
♦ Formative Strategies

After you have completed one assessment and know the routine, you can quickly go to the *Full Procedure* section in subsequent assessments. Once students have completed the assessment, you will have a student baseline for this assessment.

Each assessment contains a list of possible speaking topics both on the assessment overview page and in the Speaking Topic part of each assessment. Please remind students that they can enlarge or vary the initial topic. For example, the topic of *nature* can become *things I do outdoors, camping, animals in nature, my favorite lake, a boat trip*, or *a walk to the lake*. Feel free to vary the speaking topics based on the topics covered in your curriculum. Have two different topics for the initial assessment (one for each of the two students) and two different topics for additional practice.

Keep to the time limits for the assessments, usually one minute per student, so you have a firm baseline for their future speaking. You might want to write the starting time on the board to be sure when their finishing time is. If you wish to increase the speaking time, such as to one and a half minutes, consistently use that time limit for any additional practice and retesting on that assessment.

Your first speaking formative assessment will take the longest since the students are learning the procedure. Afterwards, they can get in their pairs quickly and begin. You can refer to the *Full Procedure* for the list of speaking topics and start the speaking assessment.

You can decide if you want your students to have the same speaking partner for multiple speaking assessments or if you want the students to switch partners. Likewise, if students are in their usual speaking pairs, they can keep their assignments as Student 1 and Student 2. Also, you can decide if you want the students to have thirty seconds of think time before they begin to speak. To have reliable data for change, you should use the same format each day for the particular assessment.

If you want to use the Standard Speaking Assessment Form (Figure 3.2, page 48), students just have to add the assessment name and perhaps one or two items in the Numbers cell. However, a few assessments have their own specific forms. When using the Standard Speaking Assessment Form, remember to make copies ahead of time. You will only need half as many sheets as you have students in the class. Twenty-eight students require only fourteen copies. If you print the forms double-sided, those fourteen sheets can be used for two different assessments. If there is an odd number of students, you can partner with a student. When students complete one side, they record their information in their own speaking logs and hand in the assessment sheets so you can record and diagnose. Return the sheets when you do the next assessment.

These assessments measure where the students are in the language acquisition speaking process. They allow the students to improve so that they can be prepared for authentic speaking.

Improvement

Although it takes only two minutes for each of the students to do the initial talking, it can take thirty seconds of feedback for each (one minute more) and another thirty seconds each to practice the feedback (one minute more) for a total of four minutes (Figure 3.1). This baseline data information allows you to determine the students' present speaking status for the specific language function. If the students have received peer feedback, have practiced it, and still do not demonstrate sufficient improvement according to your established criteria, then share the formative strategies with them (*Formative Strategies* section). Each assessment has an average of ten different improvement strategies. These strategies are worded for the students so you can copy and give the information to the students. The learners will select new strategies and practice them numerous times. Then they can be reassessed on the original topic.

Already Proficient Students

Those students who demonstrate their proficiency in the first assessment can still show improvement. For example, they can set a goal of saying twenty percent more sentences in the target language. If a student said ten sentences about a given topic, she sets her goal to say twenty percent more or twelve sentences next time. Likewise, the proficient student can set a goal of including additional vocabulary about the topic; for example, a student can learn the names of additional desserts as he describes what he likes to eat. If both students in a pair show proficiency, they can both do the extension activities.

Authentic Language

Ideally, teachers should assess students based on how fluent speakers of the target language would speak in their daily lives. The language tasks in

FIGURE 3.1 Assessment and Improvement Time

	Student 1	*Student 2*
Speaks during assessment	1 minute	1 minute
Receives feedback	30 seconds	30 seconds
Practices feedback	30 seconds	30 seconds
Total	2 minutes	2 minutes

this book revolve around common daily situations, such as comparing two restaurants, asking questions about a sports event, or describing a favorite TV show. Furthermore, these formative assessments focus on essential language functions that promote real-life language use, such as socializing and giving opinions. Since these formative assessments evaluate where students are in their language acquisition for a specific language function, the assessments capture a focused snapshot of language use.

Presentational and Interpersonal Speaking

Although the following assessments are formatted as peer assessments, you can use the same form to assess any student. You can listen to the student, indicate how well he/she spoke, and provide the student with formative feedback that enables the student to instantly improve. If you assess the student, you can not only give the usual feedback but you can also provide him or her with an alternative strategy.

Most of the speaking activities in this book involve one student speaking to another student who listens and gives feedback for improvement. Therefore, the speaking activities are presentational. The assessments center on how well an individual can do by himself or herself without a speaking partner. Often the speaking performance of a student can change depending on the partner since the partner may give verbal support or may hinder the conversation. Once each individual student is assessed, is given formative feedback for improvement, and has practiced that improvement, then both students can be assessed in interpersonal speaking on the same topics by using the same assessment.

Speaking Assessments (Arranged by ACTFL Proficiency Guidelines)

FIGURE 3.2 Standard Speaking Assessment Form

Assessment: _____ Date: _____

	Student 1	Student 2
Topic		
Number		
Improve		
New strategy		
Practice topics		
Reassess		
Number (original topic)		

Basic Identification Using Vocabulary

Purpose: To orally identify as many words as possible about a given topic
Level: Novice
Speaking Type: Presentational
Grouping: Groups of two
Form: Figure 3.3 Basic Identification Using Vocabulary Assessment Form
(page 50)

Full Procedure

Explain to the students that Student 1 will start by saying as many words as possible about the general topic in one minute. Student 1 can say any related words. For example, for the topic of shopping, he/she may include such items as types of stores, items in a store, price words, and products.

After you tell Student 1 the first topic and say "Start," Student 1 has one minute to say vocabulary words related to the topic. Student 2 writes down the vocabulary topic, listens and makes a slash (/) for each word that he/she considers comprehensible and meaningful to the topic. After a minute, Student 2 converts the slashes to a number (/ / / = 3), reports that number to Student 2 and then, for the next half minute, offers additional words about the topic to Student 1, who writes down those words under the "Improve" section of the form.

Next, the students reverse roles. Give Student 2 a different speaking topic and say "Start." Student 2 talks for a minute while Student 1 listens and records. After Student 1 tallies the words and writes down the number total, he/she offers additional words to Student 2, who writes down each new word under the "Improve" section of the form.

Implementing Formative Feedback

After you collect this assessment form, monitor each student's baseline. Scan the papers to identify those students who were already proficient according to your predetermined criteria or have become proficient due to peer assessment. Share the *Formative Strategies* with those students who have a learning gap in this area. Those students select a new strategy, practice that strategy with random topics over several class periods, and then are reassessed using the original topic.

Extension

Once students have created a vocabulary list for a specific topic, such as *school*, they can use it to perform many language functions, such as asking and answering questions about their school day, narrating what happens during school, and comparing different experiences from the same day.

FIGURE 3.3 Basic Identification Using Vocabulary Assessment Form

Assessment: _____ *Date:* _____

Vocabulary: _____

	Student 1	*Student 2*
Topic		
Number		
Improve		
New strategy		
Practice topics		
Reassess		
Number (original topic)		

Speaking Topics
First topics: school, home
Second topics: family, sports/leisure time activities
Third topics: seasons, friends

Formative Strategies for Basic Identification Using Vocabulary

Read over a vocabulary word list on the given topic from your notes, a hand-out, the textbook, or a website and determine which words you did not previously say. Say out loud several times any word you did not include from the written list. Then, without looking at any list, say as many words as you can about the topic. Make a slash for each word you say.

For words that you did not remember from the topical vocabulary list, create a mental image of the word using its sound or a very closely-related sound. For example, for the Spanish word *acuerdo* (to agree), visualize two smiling people walking side by side holding *a cord*.

As you look over each vocabulary word, do an action to help you remember it. For the verb "to write," you can pretend to move an invisible pen in your hand. As you move your invisible pen, say "to write" in the target language.

Make picture flashcards (picture on one side, target language on the other) for all the words in the vocabulary topic of *sports* or *hobbies*. You can use simple line drawings, such as a shoe and ball to indicate soccer. Go through the cards several times. Then, without looking at the cards, see how many words you can say. Pull out the cards you did not remember and then practice with those several times. Then, without looking at the cards, see how many words you can say about the topic.

Look at a picture of the topic, such as a picture of a house, or think of a mental image of your house. Identify all the words related to house from the picture or image.

Speak from your experience. For example, for the topic of *travel*, think of the last family vacation you took. Then say all of the words you can think of about that trip.

You may be able to identify vocabulary for a topic more easily if you separate all words into four categories: 1) nouns (objects, people, places), 2) adjectives (descriptive words), 3) verbs (actions), and 4) other words for the topic.

Make a column for each category and write words in the appropriate column. Practice with the topic of *community/neighborhood*.

$\wp$

Think of the various categories of vocabulary within the original topic. List the categories and then say the words in those categories. For example, for the topic of *food*, you can think of fruits, vegetables, meat, drinks, and desserts. Then say all the fruit words before going on to next category. You may want to make a web or concept map to help you visualize all the categories and words in each category. Practice with the topic of *family life*.

$\wp$

Think of the first thing that pops into your brain about the given topic and begin saying all the words connected to it. When you run out of connections, let another idea pop into your brain and say words associated with that part of the topic. Practice with the topic of *house*.

$\wp$

Practice by "zooming out" and "zooming in" on a certain word. When you zoom out, think of what other categories the word belongs to. For example, when you zoom out on *carrot*, you might think of the topic *vegetables*, the broader topic *food*, and the even broader topic *eating*. You can zoom in by thinking of more and more specific categories. For the topic of *carrot*, you could start with a general description, then color, then texture. Pick a topic such as *shopping* and practice zooming in or out. Count your words. Then think of what other words you could have said. Do the same vocabulary topic again and count your words.

$\wp$

For a "one degree of separation" activity, say as many words as you can that are connected to the given original topic. For example, for the topic of *shopping*, you can say the names of clothing, places you shop, people you talk to while shopping, transportation for shopping, and occupations. You might make a concept map or web to think through connected ideas. Practice with the topic of *job*.

$\wp$

Learning cognates is a great way to increase your vocabulary in a target Romance language such as French or Italian. For example, the English word *student* is *studente* in Italian. Pick a topic and try to find as many cognates as you can that relate to it.

$\wp$

With a partner who wants to improve on basic identification using vocabulary, work together to create picture flashcards (target word on one side and a picture on the other). As your partner holds up cards with the image facing you, say the words associated with them. The partner will look at the back of the card to see if you are correct and help you learn more vocabulary. Then reverse roles to help your partner practice.

$\bigcirc$

Review your current vocabulary words with online flashcards such as those at proprofs.com or through PowerPoint presentations. For example, you can search for German Restaurant vocabulary PowerPoint to find vocabulary practice.

Socializing Function: Greetings

Purpose: To socialize by asking as many personal questions as possible
Level: Novice
Speaking Type: Presentational
Grouping: Groups of two
Form: Standard Speaking Assessment Form

Full Procedure

Explain to the students that Student 1 will start by asking as many greeting questions (questions you would ask someone you just met) as possible in one minute. The goal is for Student 1 to find out as much as possible about Student 2.

After you tell Student 1 the first topic and say "Start," he/she has a minute to ask questions that he/she would normally ask when greeting someone for the first time. Student 2 listens and records each personal question with a slash. If Student 2 does not understand the statement or question or does not feel that it is a greeting type question, he/she does not record it. After a minute, Student 2 tallies the slashes, records the total, and tells Student 1 how many greeting questions he/she asked.

They reverse roles. After you tell Student 2 the first topic and say "Start," Student 2 has a minute to ask questions. After a minute, Student 1 tallies the slashes, records the total, and tells Student 2 how many greeting questions he/she asked.

After both students have spoken, they collectively try to think of more questions to ask someone who they meet for the first time. They record these additional questions in the "Improve" section. Then, they practice using the additional questions.

Implementing Formative Feedback

After you collect this assessment form, monitor each student's baseline. Scan the collected papers to identify those students who were already proficient according to your predetermined criteria or have become proficient due to peer assessment. Share the *Formative Strategies* with those students who have a learning gap in this area. Those students select a new strategy, practice that strategy with random topics over several class periods, and then are reassessed using the original topic.

Extension

To change this assessment into a conversation, Student 2 answers after Student 1 asks a socializing question. Also, the students can reorder the socializing questions to follow a more normal flow of conversation. For example, people usually ask someone's name before they ask where they live. Furthermore, after Student 2 answers, Student 1 can ask a clarifying question or react ("I live near there!").

Formative Strategies for Socializing Function: Greetings

Identify different categories that you can include in your greeting questions such as health, name, and home location. What other common categories do you use in a "greeting" conversation? Practice asking at least one question for each category to a partner.

Make a list of the questions you would ask someone who you have not seen recently—a friend you saw an hour ago, a family friend you have not seen in a long while, a relative you have not seen for several years, or a complete stranger. Compare these lists to identify all the possible different types of questions you might ask. Then, out loud, go through each of these encounters with a partner.

Think of what questions a friend asked you the last time you met. Ask those questions in the target language to a partner.

Draw a symbol on one side of a 3 × 5 card for a common greeting question and, on the back of the card, write the question. Create ten cards. For example, you may have a birthday cake on one side and "How old are you?" on the other. Next, show your symbol cards to your partner who answers the questions while you check his/her answers. Then your partner shows his/her symbols as you say the questions and your partner checks your answers.

Write out a list of ten important questions to ask anyone that you meet for the first time. Practice asking these questions to a partner without looking at the list. Your partner will answer the questions. Then switch.

Think of the five W questions (*Who, What, Where, When,* and *Why*), plus *Which, How* and *How Many*. Ask a partner a greeting question with each of these to find out more about him/her.

Listen to a digital conversation that your teacher or a classmate has recorded previously using a program such as Audacity. Identify each greeting question and repeat that question. Then use those questions to help you as you ask questions of your partner.

With another student who wants to improve in this area of socializing, play "Who am I?" Each person thinks of a famous person from a TV show, a book, a sport, etc. Student 1 asks greeting questions to figure out who Student 2's mystery person is. Student 1 is not allowed ask "What is your name?" Then reverse roles.

Some different ways of thinking about questions to ask someone:

- Become a detective who is interviewing a person at a crime scene. How much can you find out about the person through your questions? Do with a partner.
- At a party, you just were introduced to a person you think you like. Find out as much as you can about the person to determine if you want to ask the person out. Do with a partner.
- You are invited to a speed dating event. Write down all the questions you want to ask and practice asking those questions quickly since you only have a limited time with each person. Do one speed dating with a partner.

Other strategy suggested by the teacher or peers:

Basic Information Using Sentences

Purpose: To say as much basic information using as many sentences about a given topic as possible
Level: Intermediate
Speaking Type: Presentational
Grouping: Groups of two
Form: Standard Speaking Assessment Form

Full Procedure

Explain to the students that Student 1 will start by saying as many basic information sentences as possible about a topic in one minute. Student 1 will think of the topic, such as *store*, in a very general manner; he/she can include such things as types of store, items in a store, description of item prices, and actions done in any store.

After you tell Student 1 the first topic (see the listing after the form) and say "Start," Student 1 says sentences related to the topic for one minute. Student 2 writes down the topic, listens, and makes a slash (/) for each sentence that he/she considers comprehensible and meaningful to the topic. After a minute, Student 2 converts the slashes to a number (/ / / = 3), reports that number to Student 2 and, then, for the next half minute, offers additional sentences about the topic to Student 1, who writes down those sentences under the "Improve" section of the form.

Then these students reverse roles. Give Student 2 a different topic, and say "Start." Student 2 talks for a minute while Student 1 listens and records. After Student 1 tallies the sentences and writes down the number total, he/she offers additional sentences to Student 2 who writes down each new sentence under the "Improve" section of the form.

Implementing Formative Feedback

After you collect this assessment form, monitor each student's baseline. Scan the papers to identify those students who were already proficient according to your predetermined criteria or have become proficient due to peer assessment. Share the *Formative Strategies* with those students who have a learning gap in this area. Those students select a new strategy, practice that strategy with random topics over several class periods, and then are reassessed using the original topic.

Extension

As a follow-up, the students can redo the assessment by putting their sentences into a logical order to narrate something about the topic. For example, using the topic of *my favorite store*, they can narrate what happens from when they enter the store to when they leave it. Also, as a student talks about the topic, his/her partner can ask questions or give more information. The pair of students can compete to see who can come up with the most information about a topic or person.

Speaking Topics
First topics: your favorite season, an interesting TV show or movie
Second topics: good things about your town/neighborhood, going
    shopping/stores
Third topics: clothing, weekend

Formative Strategies for Basic Information Using Sentences

Whatever enters your head as you think of the topic, talk about it as much as you can before moving on to the next. For example, for the topic of *clothing*, start by talking about your shirt/blouse. Give all details about the shirt/blouse before describing your pants/skirt. Practice with the topic of *celebration* or *holiday*.

Use Langrehr's SCUMPS (Size, Color, Use, Material, Parts, Shape, other) to describe an object (2001). Tell each thing about a particular noun before you go on. Do this for *an animal* or *an object in your house*.

If you do not know a specific vocabulary word in the target language, use a more general word instead (use *meat* if you cannot remember *steak* and use *clothing* for the more specific word *shirt*) or another word that expresses a similar action (say *walk* when you cannot remember *run* and say *eat* if you cannot remember *chew*). As you think of the keywords for the topic of *this evening*, say sentences using more general words or synonyms for each keyword.

Narrow the topic down (zoom in) to a specific, very familiar aspect of it. For example, for the topic of *school*, think of being in your favorite classroom and zoom in on doing your favorite activity in that class. Then talk about that activity. Narrow down the topic of *leisure activities* so that you can talk about it.

Tell a story about something that happens within a topic, such as *a funny thing that happened last weekend*. Say many different sentences when you tell the sequence of the story.

$\wp$

Give more than just the details about a topic. Give your opinion about it. If you are talking about an object, say when you use it. For example, for the topic *shirt*, you can say, "My shirt is red. I really like the shirt. It goes well with my red hair. I wear it when I go to dances." Practice with the topic of *being invited to a party*.

$\wp$

Think of all the actions (verbs) associated with a topic. Put them in a logical order. For example, for the topic of *shopping*, you may organize your verbs into a logical order: enter, look, ask, try on, look in mirror, dislike, find another, like, and pay. Then add some additional information to each verb to create a complete sentence, such as "I enter the store to buy a blouse." Practice with the actions for *a family vacation*.

$\wp$

Picture the given topic in your mind. For example, with the topic of *house*, create a mental picture of your house and the things that happen in it. Tell your partner what you see: "My father is in the kitchen. He really enjoys cooking. He makes bread. He does not like to wash the dishes."

$\wp$

Make a speaking form in which you identify as many actions, objects/people, descriptions for the given topic (Figure 3.4). Then make sentences by using two or more categories, such as "In school (the place), the teacher (the person) reads (action) the big book (description)." Complete the form and say sentences for the topic of *school*.

$\wp$

With a group of other students who want to improve on Basic Information Using sentences, do a "round-robin" for the topic. You say a sentence about the topic of *my birthday* and then the next student, going clock wise, says

FIGURE 3.4 Speaking Form by Categories (Partial Listing)

Places	People/ Objects	Actions	Descriptions	Useful Expressions
the class the school . . .	the teacher the notebook the book . . .	to study to read to write . . .	hard easy big . . .	How boring! How interesting! . . .

another sentence until you have gone around the circle. After each sentence, the speaker pauses for ten seconds. Listen carefully to the different types of sentences being said and ask yourself, "Can I add this to my list of new things to say about the topic?" If another sentence has new information or a new way of describing the topic, write the sentence down during the ten-second pause. Go around the circle again and again. If a student cannot say anything, then the next student talks. Continue until no one can say any more sentences about the topic. At the end of the "round-robin," review your list of "new" sentences and use those sentence idea strategies for another topic such as *people in the community*.

With another student who wants to improve on Basic Information Using sentences, find and print out at least three pictures about the topic from your own personal pictures or those at Flickr or Google Images. For example, you may have three pictures of a basketball game. Talk as much as you can about one picture, then go to the second, and then to the third. Do this strategy for the topic of *family*.

Other strategy suggested by the teacher or peers:

Detailed Information Sentences About a Topic

Purpose: To say as many detailed information sentences about a given topic as possible

Level: Intermediate

Speaking Type: Presentational

Grouping: Groups of two

Form: Standard Speaking Assessment Form

Full Procedure

Explain to the students that Student 1 will start by saying as many detailed sentences as possible in one minute. "The shirt is red," "The shirt is green," and "The shirt is black" count as one detailed sentence, not three, since they only vary in one word. If the student receives the topic of *shopping*, he/she can say, "I shop in Vizmart. Vizmart is on Smith Road in Palmyra. I pay eight dollars for a shirt. . . . " In the previous sentences, the details are "Vizmart," "Smith Road," Palmyra," and "eight dollars"; these details supply facts about the shopping: the *who, what, where, when, how, which*, etc. Each fact has to be different.

After you tell Student 1 the first topic (see the listing after the form) and say "Start," Student 1 says detailed sentences related to the topic for one minute. Student 2 writes down the topic, listens, and makes a slash (/) for each detailed sentence that he/she considers comprehensible and meaningful to the topic. After a minute, Student 2 converts the slashes to a number (/ / / = 3), reports that number to Student 2 and, then, for the next half minute, helps change non-factual statements into factual ones and offers several more in-depth sentences about the topic while Student 1 writes down those words under the "Improve" section of the form.

Next, the students reverse roles. Give Student 2 a different topic, and say "Start." Student 2 gives detailed information about the topic for one minute while Student 1 listens and records. After Student 1 tallies the sentences and writes down the number total, he/she offers additional sentences to Student 2, who writes down each new word under the "Improve" section of the form. Then both students spend a minute collectively thinking about what other details or facts they can add next time. They put these in the "Improve" section of the form.

Implementing Formative Feedback

After you collect this assessment form, monitor each student's baseline. Scan the papers to identify those students who were already proficient according to your predetermined criteria or have become proficient due to peer assessment. Share the *Formative Strategies* with those students who have a learning gap in this area. Those students select a new strategy, practice that strategy with random topics over several class periods, and then are reassessed using the original topic.

Extension

Next, the students re-say their sentences in a logical order. Also, as one student speaks, the other asks questions, reacts, or gives more information. Role play a police officer who is telling all the details of the event to his/her boss.

Speaking Topics
First topics: a difficult class, description of my favorite food/restaurant
Second topics: information about nature/outdoors, planning a trip
Third topics: daily actions, a job/career

Formative Strategies for Detailed Information Sentences About a Topic

To practice, use a mini-form and say as many different details as possible by substituting different words in each slot. For example, use "At (time) _____, I (action) _____ in (place) _____" to generate as many sentences as possible on a single topic. For the topic of *daily activities*, you might say, "At six o'clock, I wash in the bathroom. At seven o'clock I eat in the kitchen."

Mentally ask the five Ws (*who, what, where, when,* and *why*) plus *which, how,* and *how many* about the topic and then answer at least one question word in each sentence. For the topic of *the neighborhood* say, "The tall man lives here (Who?). He drives a blue car (What?). He goes fast (How?)" Tell more about your neighborhood.

Ask a partner to check your sentences against this use of details as you talk about the topic of *summer* or *my friend*.

- ○ name of the person(s)
- ○ different actions
- ○ location(s)
- ○ time (hour, day, month season, year)
- ○ reason for doing something

- way of doing it
- numbers
- colors
- names of objects or things
- descriptions of people, things, and places
- opinions/preferences

Your partner will tell you which of these you included and did not include. Say a sentence for each you did not include. Then your partner talks about the other topic.

Use a different action (verb) in each sentence. For example, for the topic of *the neighborhood*, you can think of actions such as *drive* and *play*. Use other verbs as you talk about your neighborhood. Your partner will make sure each verb is different.

Use adjectives (descriptive words) and adverbs (-ly) that give details. Add the adjective *old* to *the man* to form "the old man" and add *slowly* to *talks* to produce "the old man talks slowly." Practice adding an adjective or adverb to each short sentence to give it more detail about the topic of *buying clothing*.

As you say a sentence on the topic of *healthy foods*, your partner will add more detail to each of your sentences. For example, if you say, "Salads are healthy," your partner adds, "Salads with fruit are healthy." Listen to the details your partner adds and try to include more details in your subsequent sentences. Say ten sentences. Then your partner talks about *horrible food*.

Think of something that you or someone else has done with a part of this topic and tell that story with all its details. For example, for the topic of *travel*, think of how you and your friends got lost going someplace. Tell about each detail of that adventure (Who was on the trip? What did they wear? When was it?).

Think of someone famous (from real life, TV/movie, or a book) or someone you know who has done something with this topic. For example, for the topic of *travel*, think of a TV show such as "The Amazing Race" in which people travel and you retell the TV show. Share your sentences for the topic of *travel* with a partner who will talk about the topic of *vacation*.

Pretend you are a sports announcer who tells each detail that is happening during a basketball game. For example, "Tom gets the brown ball. He quickly runs down the court. He looks around. He throws it to John. John makes three points." You can be a sports announcer for any event or situation, such as a family supper or a trip to the mall. Make sure to give a detailed account.

Work with another student who wants to improve on giving detailed information. One of you says a basic sentence such as "I walk." The other person adds one more detail to it such as "I walk in the park." Then add more: "I walk in the park with John." Continue until no one can add any more details to the sentence. Enlarge the basic sentences of "I study," "I go to class," and "I talk" for the topic of *my first class*.

Other strategy suggested by the teacher or peers:

Reflex Grammar About a Topic

Purpose: To say as many full sentences about a topic as possible by using a specific grammar concept
Level: Intermediate
Speaking Type: Presentational
Grouping: Groups of two
Form: Standard Speaking Assessment Form

Full Procedure

Explain to the students that Student 1 will start by saying as many sentences or questions about the topic as possible using a specific grammar form. For example, if Student 1 is given the topic of *weekend* and the grammatical form of *future*, then that student might say, "I will walk to the lake" and "I will swim for an hour." Remember to try to tell a story by using full sentences that contain more than just the subject and verb.

After you tell Student 1 the first topic and say "Start," Student 1 proceeds to say as many sentences about the topic as possible using the assigned grammatical concept. Student 1 speaks for 1 minute while Student 2 listens and records each sentence with a slash. If Student 2 does not understand the sentence, does not feel that it is grammatically correct, or does not think it is full sentence (not just "I will swim," but "I will swim in the lake."), then he/she does not record a slash. At the end of a minute, the partner converts the slashes to a number (/ / / / = 4), writes down the number, and reports that number to the first student. Student 2 suggests some additional sentences or corrects sentences that Student 1 writes down in the "Improve" section of the form. They reverse roles with a different topic. Student 1 listens, makes the slashes, records the total number, and reports the information to the partner. Student 1 suggests some additional sentences or corrections which Student 1 writes down in the "Improve" section.

Implementing Formative Feedback

After you collect this assessment form, monitor each student's baseline. Scan the papers to identify those students who were already proficient according to your predetermined criteria or have become proficient due to peer assessment. Share the *Formative Strategies* with those students who have a learning gap in this area. Those students select a new strategy, practice that strategy with random topics over several class periods, and then are reassessed using the original topic.

Extension

Students can move from this exercise to a conversation. For example, their partners can react to each statement by asking questions such as "With whom will you go snowboarding?" or "Will you snowboard for one or two days?" In addition, as the speaker says a sentence, the partner responds to each by agreeing or disagreeing. Likewise, their partner can react by listening to all the sentences and then telling his/her version of a similar situation.

Speaking Topics

First topics: describe the objects in the class (adjective agreement), tell the things your friend does today (third person present verb form)

Second topics: compare two places to eat (adjective comparison), tell what you will do when you are 21 (future tense)

Third topics: talk about your house (possessive adjectives), express your thoughts about the next sports game (affirmative and negative expressions)

Formative Strategies for Reflex Grammar About a Topic

Think about the given topic, such as *family*, and then review grammar, such as adjective comparison, by looking at your handouts, textbook, or a website. Some websites like Quia have grammar practices. For example, you may say "My father is taller than my mother." After you have read, understood the examples, and practiced them, then say sentences using adjective comparisons for the topic of *the differences in my family*.

Think about the topic of *my weekend* and the preterit tense. Make a quick "cheat sheet" in which you write down any irregular verbs or grammatical forms and what the correct form is. For example, you identify the verb form "I speak → I spoke." You may write down any memory technique that will help you to remember the irregular past form. For example, you may use a mental image such as visualizing a person in old clothing speaking through the spokes of a wagon wheel (I speak → I spoke). Tell your weekend story using the past tense including the irregulars.

For your topic of *comparing two clothing stores*, make a quick chart of the pros and cons of each store (the comparisons). Then write the pros and cons out as sentences. Look the sentences over to see if they are correct by comparing them to your handout, textbook, or a website. You may ask a peer or the teacher to look them over. Then, without looking at the written sentences, say the sentences in a logical order, such as all the good things about the first store, then all the bad things about the second store.

If you are having trouble saying full sentences for your topic and the grammar of the future tense, start out by only saying the future tense verb. For example, just say the future tense of the verbs, such as "I will study," from your picture verb flashcards. Then once you are sure you are saying the future tense correctly, give additional information such as "I will study history in the library" to create a more detailed sentence for the topic of *school*. Start with simple verb phrases and then enlarge to full sentences to say your narration of *tomorrow at school*.

If you are speaking about the topic of *yesterday* in the past tense, take out your picture verb flashcards and select the ones that fit the exercise, such as the irregular past tense. Go through the cards as quickly as you can by saying that tense correctly and relating the verbs to the given topic. For example, for the topic of *house*, you may say "I left school" and "I went to my house." Then go through the cards again, verbally adding more information as you go; change the "leave" visual flashcard to the basic sentence of "I left" and then to the fuller sentence of "I left school at two o'clock." Rearrange the order of the picture verb flashcards so that you can retell the story of what happened yesterday in a logical order.

Work with a peer who wants to improve in this area of reflex grammar. Say several sentences about the topic *party* using the verb tense you are currently studying in class. As you speak, your partner will give you a thumbs up (correct conjugation) or a thumbs down (incorrect conjugation) for each sentence. At the end, retry the incorrect sentences. If you need help saying the correct verb form, ask your partner to tell you or look in your textbook.

Work with a peer who wants to improve in this area of reflex grammar. Use Figure 3.5 Peer Assisted Reflex (page 68) to ask questions, record typical answers, and reference helpful hints for your or your partner if one of you makes a mistake. Practice answering questions using the correct form of verbs, such as the past tense of "to do." Then switch roles and use the chart to ask your partner questions.

As your partner does a series of six or more actions, quickly tell a story using the appropriate grammar. For example, your partner acts out getting ready for school as you quickly say the reflexive verbs such as "I get (myself) up." In another activity, your partner can pretend to give objects to various students as you practice using direct and indirect objects. For example, "He gives her the book," and "He gives them the pens."

FIGURE 3.5 Peer Assisted Reflex

Student 2: Ask your partner the question below. Do not let him/her see this paper unless he/she is having difficulty. As he/she answers, check the right column.	Common responses. Student 2: If your partner does not have an answer similar to these answers, help him/her by giving them the Hints.
Did you go to the beach a week ago?	Yes, I went to the beach a week ago. No, I did not go to the beach. No, I didn't go to the beach. Hint: Answer in the "I" form when you are asked a "you" question. Hint: Answer in the past tense (did). Hint: Either use "did" + verb ("did go") or put the verb in the past tense ("went").

You may be able to do a speaking activity, such as *a description of the mall*, more easily if you use an acronym (an abbreviation or word that is formed using the initial letters of a phrase or name) to help you remember how to use the grammar form correctly. For example, you may use the acronym "LITE," Location, Illness, Temporary, Emotion, to recall when to use the Spanish verb *estar* as opposed to the verb *ser*, both which translate as "to be" (Center for Advanced Research on Language Acquisition, 2010). Search the internet for acronym+Language+a specific grammar point such as acronym+French+adjective or make up your own acronym for the grammar point and then then use it to help you talk about the topic *your time in the park*.

Communicate the events of a family trip and focus on using the grammar reflex for possessive adjectives. First, do a practice run by saying a sentence for each possessive form, such as *my, your, his, her, our,* and *their*. Then rearrange the sentences to tell a story. For example, you can say, "My father drives our car . . . Carla listens to her music . . . I watch my video. " Your partner checks not only for the correct forms but for whether or not you give additional information about the trip. Next, your partner uses possessives with the topic of *my friends*.

Other strategy suggested by the teacher or peers:

Asking Questions and Giving Information

Purpose: To engage in a conversation by asking and answering information questions about a given topic

Level: Intermediate

Speaking Type: Interpersonal

Grouping: Groups of two

Form: Figure 3.6 Asking Questions and Giving Information Assessment Form (page 71)

Full Procedure

Explain to the students that Student 1 will start by asking an information question about the topic. Student 2 will answer it by giving more information about the topic or asking Student 1 a different question. If either partner asks a question and the other student does not respond in five seconds, then you can either answer your own question or ask another question.

After you tell Student 1 the first topic (see the Speaking Topics listing) and say "Start," Student 1 starts by asking a question. He/she self-records a slash under "Student 1: Number of Questions Asked." Since both students are speaking, each records his/her own questions and answers. If Student 2 answers that question, he/she records a slash under "Student 2: Number of Questions Answered." If Student 2 gives even more information about the answer, he/she records another slash under "Student 2: Number of Questions Answered." If Student 2 asks another question about the topic, then he/she records a slash under "Student 2: Number of Questions Asked." If the partner does not say anything after a five second pause, the other partner can ask a different question. They speak for two minutes.

At the end, they convert the slashes to numbers (// = 2). For a minute, both students list what they could do to ask more questions and answer them. They write these in the "Improve" cells.

Implementing Formative Feedback

After you collect this assessment form, monitor each student's baseline. Scan the papers to identify those students who need additional assistance and those who are already proficient. Share the *Formative strategies* with those who have a learning gap in this area. The students select one new strategy, practice that chosen strategy with random topics over several class periods, and then are reassessed using the original topic.

Extension

Next, the students can arrange their questions in a logical order in which a person might ask them, instead of the random order in which they probably asked them initially. Then they redo their asking and answering the questions. Also, they can collaborate to think of different questions to ask and answer about the topic.

Speaking Topics

First topics: asking a friend for money, finding out about the daily activities of an exchange student

Second topics: asking a boss about your new job, discovering information about a new student

Third topics: celebrations/holidays, seasons

Formative Strategies for Asking Questions and Giving Information

Work with another student who wants to improve in the area of asking questions and giving information. Play "Question Tag" in which you ask your partner a question about a topic; your partner answers it and asks another question using the same question word or verb form. For example, if you ask a "Where" question about the *game* topic such as "Where do you play baseball?" your partner answers that question and also uses "Where" in another question such as "Where do you go after the game?" Play this game until neither of you can say any different questions for the same question word and for this topic then move on to a different question word. Talk about your favorite sport.

$\bigcirc$

Pick one important object, place, or person from current events. Ask as many questions about it as you can before you move on to the next important object, place, or person. For example, you may ask as much as you can about a country in general before you move on to questions about its leader. Practice asking questions about a current event with a partner. Be sure to use critical question words like "Who," "Where," "Why," and "What next?"

$\bigcirc$

To be better at answering questions, remember that each question word corresponds with a specific answer (Who: person or group; What: object or thing; Where: location; When: time [hour, day, month, season, year]; Why: a reason [because . . .] ; Which: a specific thing or person; How many: a number; and How: condition, manner, or explanation). Practice giving the answers for questions about *problems at the hotel* with these relationships in mind. For each question word, practice asking a question and giving an appropriate answer.

$\bigcirc$

FIGURE 3.6 Asking Questions and Giving Information Assessment Form

Assessment: _____ *Date:* _____

	Student 1	*Student 2*
Topic		
Number: Questions Asked		
Number: Questions Answered		
Improve		
New strategy		
Practice topics		
Reassess		
Number (original topic)		

Work with another student who wants to improve in the area of asking questions and giving information. Ask each other questions and practice in responding to the questioner by using questions like "And you?" or "Do you think it is true?" or by giving reaction statements such as "Really?" or "Why?" or "Tell me more." Practice with the topic of *the best team*.

$\wp$

When answering a question, pay special attention to the verb form of your answer. If you are asked a question about yourself, you answer in the "I" form. For example, you could respond, "Yes, I have two brothers" to the question "Do you have any brothers?" Likewise, if you are asked a question about what "he," "she," or "they" do, use the same verb form in the answer (e.g., "Does your sister play baseball?"/"Yes, my sister does play baseball." or "Did her team win?"/"Yes, the team did win."). Practice listening to the verb form in each question so that you can more easily answer it. Have another student who wants to improve in this area ask you questions using "you," "he," "she," and "they" so that you can answer them accordingly. Then ask your partner the same type of questions. Practice with the topic of *finding out about an upcoming concert*.

$\wp$

When responding to a question, you can often answer in a shorter form since the original question had the important information. You can use a simple sentence instead of a full, complex sentence. For example, you can answer the question "Who won the game at the arena last night?" with "We won." Likewise, for the question "Where did she go last night after the dance?" answer with "She went home." With a partner, practice asking a question and giving a short answer about a movie you disliked.

$\wp$

Think about three types of asking questions: open-ended, close-ended, and evaluative. Asking open-ended questions or divergent questions which have many possible answers promotes more talking than closed-ended questions or convergent questions which only have one answer. For example, the open-ended questions, "Why do you like to swim?" or "How do you make a sandwich?" promote a wide range of possible answers; closed-ended questions, such as "When do you arrive at school?" or "What is the date?" require a short, specific answer. Likewise, an evaluative question asks the listener to think through the reasons for something such as "How are Washington DC and Rome, Italy similar?" For the topic of *the mall*, ask one closed-ended question, three open-ended questions, and two evaluative questions.

$\wp$

You can make your questions climb from a low level of thinking and speaking to a very high level of thinking and speaking. The higher levels prompt more talking. The following sample questions are arranged from low level to high level:

- Knowledge: Where is . . . ? When is . . . ? Who is . . . ?
- Comprehension: How would you describe . . . ? Can you explain . . . ? How would you summarize . . . ?
- Application: How would you solve . . . ? What questions would you ask in an interview with . . . ?
- Analysis: How are these similar? How are these different? How is this related to that?
- Synthesis: What if . . . ? What solutions do you have for the problem of . . . ? How would you create a new . . . ?
- Evaluation: Do you believe . . . ? Why . . . ? What is the best . . . ? How do you prioritize . . . ?

Ask a question for each level for the topic of *a family activity*.

Other strategy suggested by the teacher or peers:

Maintaining Conversations Through Prompts

Purpose: To be able to maintain a conversation through prompted questions, topics, or subtopics
Level: Intermediate
Speaking Type: Interpersonal
Grouping: Groups of two
Form: Figure 3.7 Maintaining Conversations Through Prompts

Full Procedure

Explain to the students that Student 1 and Student 2 will maintain a conversation for three minutes about a certain situation by using written conversation prompts. For any written prompt, they are to express the general idea, not the word-for-word translation. For example, if the prompt is "Order a hamburger," students could say sentences like "I want a hamburger," "I would like to have a hamburger," or "A hamburger, please."

Look at the prompt cards (Figure 3.8, page 76, and Figure 3.9, page 77) to make sure they are appropriate for your students' level. If not, you or your students can write different prompts. Give Student 1 the first prompt card and Student 2 the second prompt card, then say "Start." Student 1 will read the first prompt on his/her card and respond with a sentence. Then Student 2 responds to his/her first prompt sentence. If Student 2 considers Student 1's sentence to be comprehensible and meaningful, he/she circles the number "1" under Student 1's number column (Figure 3.7). Likewise, Student 1 circles "1" if Student 2 says a comprehensible and meaningful sentence. They continue through all the numbered prompts on their cards. If a student cannot answer a particular prompt, he/she may skip to the next one. At the end of three minutes, the students look at how many successful sentences they said and offer each other suggestions on ways to respond to the unanswered prompts, other ways to answer, and how to make answers more grammatically correct. The students record these suggestions and ideas under their "Improve" sections in the form.

Implementing Formative Feedback

After you collect the assessment forms, monitor each student's baseline. Scan the papers to identify those students who were already proficient according to your predetermined criteria or have become proficient due to peer assessment. Share the *Formative Strategies* with those students who have a learning gap in this area. Those students select a new strategy, practice that strategy

FIGURE 3.7 Maintaining Conversations Through Prompts Assessment Form

Assessment: _____ *Date:* _____

	Student 1	Student 2
Topic		
Number: *Topic 1*	Prompts 1 2 3 4 5 6 7 8 9 10	Prompts 1 2 3 4 5 6 7 8 9 10
Number: *Topic 2*	Prompts 1 2 3 4 5 6 7 8 9 10	Prompts 1 2 3 4 5 6 7 8 9 10
Number: *Topic 3*	Prompts 1 2 3 4 5 6 7 8 9 10	Prompts 1 2 3 4 5 6 7 8 9 10
Number: *Subtopics*		
Improve		
New *strategy*		
Practice *topics*		
Reassess		
Number *(original* *topic)*		

FIGURE 3.8 Prompt Card: Party

Student 1

Topic: talking with a friend at Sara's birthday party
Respond to each prompt in your own words.

1. Ask how Student 2 is.
2. Ask Student 2 if he/she sees Mary.
3. Ask when she will arrive.
4. Ask how she is getting to the party.
5. State that you like the music.
6. Ask if your friend has this type of music.
7. Ask what food they are serving at the party.
8. Ask how old Sara is.
9. Say that she has five brothers and five sisters.
10. Ask Student 2 if he/she is going to talk with Sara.

Student 2

Topic: talking with a friend at Sara's birthday party
Respond to each prompt in your own words.

1. Tell him/her that you are doing fine.
2. Respond that Mary is not here yet.
3. Say that she will arrive at 9:00 pm.
4. Answer that she has her parents' car.
5. Respond that you also like it.
6. Respond that you have many songs of this singer.
7. Say that they have hamburgers, salads, and soda.
8. Say that she is 16.
9. Comment that she has a big family.
10. Respond that you want to talk with her.

with random topics over several class periods, and then are reassessed using the original topic.

Extension

Prompted conversations provide the initial scaffolding for those students who need high structure in their speaking to maintain a conversation. The Spanish Advanced Placement exam uses a type of prompted conversation. Students can make their own conversation prompts and practice by interviewing each other. For example, students can practice by playing the parts of a reporter and a celebrity.

FIGURE 3.9 Prompt Card: Restaurant

Student 1
Topic: eating in a restaurant Respond to each prompt in your own words. Student 1 is the waiter. 1. Greet the customer formally. 2. Say that the weather is hot. 3. Ask what he/she wants to drink. 4. Ask if he/she is ready to order. 5. Describe one of the specials, such as the chicken with bananas. 6. Ask what the person wants to eat. 7. Present the customer with his/her food. 8. Ask the person if he/she likes the meal. 9. Ask the person if he/she wants some dessert. 10. Ask if the person wants more to drink.
Student 2
Topic: eating in a restaurant Respond to each prompt in your own words. Student 2 is a customer in a restaurant. 1. Greet the waiter. 2. Say that you like to swim in this weather. 3. Say that you want a soft drink. 4. Respond that you are ready. 5. Respond that you think that meal does not sound good. 6. Say that you will eat a salad. 7. Thank the waiter. 8. Say that the food is good. 9. Say that you want ice cream. 10. Say "No, thanks."

Speaking Topics

Less Structured Prompts (Subtopics)

Subtopic prompts about a sports game: preparations, actions during the
    game, feelings after the game, activities after the game

School: description of the school, classes, homework, school-related activities

Minimally Structured Prompt

You want to find out about the exchange student who will be living with you
    for the next six months. Student 1: You, Student 2: the exchange student.

Your parent (Father or Mother) is upset with how much you are spending using the family credit card.

Formative Strategies for Maintaining Conversations Through Prompts

Maintaining a conversation involves many skills such as asking follow-up questions, taking turns, reacting, requesting and giving clarification, and changing topics (Washburn and Christianson, 1995). Look at the first prompted conversation and redo it by adding turn-taking such as "And You?" or by giving strong reactions such as "What a great party!"

Another way to maintain a conversation involves asking questions. Make up ten questions about the topic of *a holiday* or *party*. Then have a partner answer your questions. Then you answer your partner's ten questions about the same topic. As a variation, answer your partner's question and ask him/her a question related to the same topic. When you have run out of questions about a subtopic, move on to another subtopic.

Work with a peer who wants to improve in this area of maintaining conversations. Pick your own topic, such as *two students trying to decide which movie to see*. Together, list the critical aspects of what makes a movie good, such as the movie title, movie genre, actor, action, and setting. Then use those as your speaking prompts for your movie conversation.

When you are given a conversation prompt, try to paraphrase rather than translate your thoughts into the target language. The goal should be to communicate the main idea of your sentences. For example, if the prompt for a clothing store says, "Say that you will buy the shirt," you might say something like, "I will take the shirt," "I want the shirt," "I like this shirt," or "I have money for the shirt." If you do not know a specific word, use a similar word or concept. Practice several different ways of saying each of these: "My boss is horrible," "We work hard," "The jobs lasts many hours," "I carry heavy things," and "There are problems at work."

Get into a group of four students who want to improve in this oral skill of maintaining conversations. Go through either of the prompted conversations line by line. Ask each student to say a variation on each line. After you have generated many variations, go through the conversation a second time. This time, each student says a variation and either adds more information or asks a question. Then get into pairs and say the various conversations.

Remember that a prompted conversation puts together ideas you have already learned in class. As soon as you see the topic, think of what you already know about it and express that knowledge in sentences. For example, if the topic is *Mary wants to exercise in a park while her friend wants to go to the gym*, think of all the things you already can say or ask about this topic. Use your previously learned sentences in the conversation.

Say what you can say; do not become frustrated when you are unable to recall a specific word. Use general words like "meat" when you cannot think of a specific meat food word like "steak"; also use words that have a similar meaning such as, if you cannot think of "walk," you say "go." Tell your partner five subtopics for the topic of *an argument with a friend* and then you two do the whole conversation including these subtopics.

Use simple sentences that you have previously learned. When you are asked what you do in September, you can identify one action, such as a sport (play football) or hobby (watch television) in a sentence such as "In September, I play football." You do not need a complex sentence such as "In the month of September when it is cool, I like to play football with my four friends in the field across from John's house." You are to say each sentence in a comprehensible and meaningful way. Think of a situation such as telling an exchange student your favorite foods and finding out his/her favorite foods. Then have this conversation with another student.

Work with a peer who wants to improve in the area of maintaining conversations. Pick your own situation like *two students talking about an upcoming game* or *two students deciding what to do after school*. Write out your prompts and then go through the conversation. Help each other make sure that the both of you can say each prompt in a comprehensible and meaningful manner. Figure out which questions open up the conversation, such as "How did you like the party?" (divergent questions), and which generate a short answer that close down a conversation, such as "What time is it?" (convergent questions). Redo the conversation with more opening-up conversation prompts.

When you are asked to speak based on just a few subtopics (*breakfast, chores, homework, sports*) or just one big topic (*my Saturday activities*), think of what you have done in topic and base the conversation on that. Have a conversation on *my Saturday activities*.

Print out four pictures from Google Images or Flickr on one topic such as *eating at a restaurant*. Put them in a logical order. Base a conversation with your partner on these pictures.

Read a teacher-created or textbook-provided conversation on a topic, such as *a trip problem*, and then, with a partner, create your own oral conversation about the same topic.

Other strategy suggested by the teacher or peers:

Inquiry with Critical Questions

Purpose: To say as many inquiries as possible using critical questions about a topic within a minute

Level: Intermediate

Speaking Type: Presentational

Grouping: Groups of two

Form: Standard Speaking Assessment Form

Full Procedure

Explain to the students that Student 1 will ask as many critical or important questions about the given topic as possible in one minute. What would someone really need to know about this topic? For example, if the student has the topic of *party*, he/she should ask important questions such as "When is the party?" and "Where is the party?" The questions have to be ones the student would realistically ask for this topic. "What color is the carpet in her living room?" would not be a critical party question.

After you tell Student 1 the first topic (see the listing after the form) and say "Start," Student 1 asks critical questions about the topic. Student 1 asks questions for 1 minute while Student 2 listens and records each critical question with a slash. If Student 2 does not understand the question or feels that it is not relevant to the topic, then he/she does not record a slash. At the end of a minute, Student 2 converts the slashes to a number (//// = 4), writes down the number, and reports that number to Student 1. Then, Student 2 suggests some additional critical questions that Student 1 writes down in the "Improve" section of the form.

Next, they reverse roles with a different topic. Student 1 tallies the slashes, records the total number, and reports the information to Student 2. Then Student 1 suggests some additional critical questions that Student 2 writes down in the "Improve" section.

Implementing Formative Feedback

After you collect this assessment form, monitor each student's baseline. Scan the papers to identify those students who were already proficient according to your predetermined criteria or have become proficient due to peer assessment. Share the *Formative Strategies* with those students who have a learning gap in this area. Those students select a new strategy, practice that strategy with random topics over several class periods, and then are reassessed using the original topic.

Extension

Next, the students can transform this into a conversation in which Student 1 ask questions, then Student 2 answers each critical question, reacts to the questions, or asks for clarification. Also, they practice asking critical questions about the topic *10 things you always wanted to know about* _____ .

Speaking Topics

First topics: a sports event or a leisure activity, a sick pet/animal
Second topics: a school problem, a city/place you want to visit
Third topics: shopping, travel/trip

Formative Strategies for Inquiry with Critical Questions

Make sure that you know the difference between critical questions and non-critical questions for your topic. You ask critical questions to find out essential information that you need to know about a given situation. If a friend tells you that there is a test, you need to know the critical information about what subject area it is, what content will be on the test, how you will answer the test (multiple choice or essay), how long the test will be, and when it is. You do not need to know what colored paper the test will be printed on or what the weather will be like outside to do well on the test. Think about some critical questions for the topic of *my ideal job*. Ask someone who also wants to improve in the area of asking critical questions to listen to your questions while you listen to his/her questions. Indicate which questions you think are critical.

As you think about the topic of *a future family vacation*, look at a list of the question words from your notes, handout, textbook or a web page. See which ones you would normally use in asking critical questions about a future family vacation and which ones you usually do not use. Make up two questions for each question word you do not normally use. Ask your questions as if you were asking your parents.

Pick a topic such as *explaining exciting places to see in the country of your target language* and ask a question for each question word. Count with your fingers to make sure you have asked the five Ws (*who, what, where, when,* and *why*), as well as *which, how many,* and *how*. If you have used all eight fingers, you have asked eight questions. For example, in talking about a job you might ask, "Who is your boss? . . . What do you do each day? . . . Where do you work?"

For any topic such as *a horrible store*, ask two different important questions for each question word. For example, for the question word *how*, you may

FIGURE 3.10 Question Words (Partial)

Question word	Many different questions
Who	Who does it? For whom does she do it? Whose book is this . . .

ask "How big is it?" "How are the clerks?" or "How much do they help you?" Practice until you can ask sixteen important different questions about the topic.

$\bigcirc$

For practice, make a form of all the question words (Figure 3.10). Then work with a partner to think of all the different questions you can ask for any question word. You may think of variations on the basic question words such as for *who*, *with whom*, *whose*, etc. Then, after you look at your form, ask these questions about the topic of *my best teacher*. Check if you used all the question words.

$\bigcirc$

Work with another student who wants to improve in the area of asking critical questions. Pick a topic such as *doing well in this language course* and ask each other critical questions about the topic. This time, start each question with a verb instead of a question word. For example, "Do you study after class?" or "Do you listen to radio stations in French?" Then, practice saying ten important verb questions about the topic of *preparing for a trip to the mountains*.

$\bigcirc$

Zoom in from the bigger topic of *shopping* to the specific task of *buying a shirt*. Once you have that smaller task in mind, you can think of important questions to ask. What questions would you ask when buying a shirt in a store?

$\bigcirc$

Before you begin to ask questions about a chosen topic, mentally review the major aspects or categories of the topic. For *fishing*, you might think of *equipment*, *boat*, *water*, and *weather*. Ask important questions about the categories for an outdoor sport.

$\bigcirc$

Practice imagining how you would act in a given situation. For the topic of *a summer trip*, think of yourself talking to a travel agent and then think of the essential questions you would ask that person about your future trip. Ask all those questions out loud.

$\bigcirc$

Work with another student who wants to improve in the area of asking critical questions. Think of critical questions for a topic such as *my neighbors*. Each of you should say your questions and then collectively decide on the ten most important questions about the topic. Then one of you can ask the questions while the other answers the questions.

The following situations may help you to think of critical questions.

♦ What critical information would you give a student from another country who is coming to your school or an out-of-towner who wants to decide which mall to go to?

♦ Pretend that you have to do a radio news report about the topic of *an interesting place in town* and you only have one minute to get all the critical information across. Think about what essential information your listeners need, such as "Where is the place?" and find out that information by asking critical questions.

♦ Think of the questions that your parents, friends, or teacher would ask you about a given topic. For example, if you went to a party but your friend did not go, what would he/she ask you?

♦ Imagine that someone has asked you to do an errand for him/her, such as going grocery shopping for one of his/her parents. What specific details do you need from that person to be able to do this errand successfully? Ask those questions.

♦ You are to make a poster about the critical information for an upcoming concert. What important information would someone want to know about the concert?

♦ You just heard about a possible job. What are some questions you would have about the job?

Other strategy suggested by the teacher or peers:

Narration/Storytelling Based on Pictures

Purpose: To narrate a story by retelling or reacting to a five-frame story or one picture

Level: Intermediate

Speaking Type: Presentational

Grouping: Groups of two

Form: Figure 3.11 Narration/Storytelling Based on Pictures Assessment Form (page 86)

Full Procedure

Explain to the students that Student 1 will narrate the picture's story in one and a half minutes. Student 1 may have one picture or a series of five pictures. This student may react to the story or retell the events of the story based on the picture(s).

After you give Student 1 the first picture story and say "Start," he/she proceeds to retell what is happening in the picture or can react to the picture in one and a half minutes (Figure 3.12, page 87). Student 2 listens and makes a slash (/) for each retelling and a slash for each reaction. Student 2 only records comprehensible and meaningful sentences. At the end of the minute, Student 2 tells Student 1 the number of sentences.

Then the students reverse roles and the process. Afterwards, they can talk over what else they could have said about or added to the picture and they write it in the "Improve" section of the form. They practice their new ideas with different topics and then are retested on the original topic.

Implementing Formative Feedback

After you collect this assessment form, monitor each student's baseline. Scan the papers to identify those students who were already proficient according to your predetermined criteria or have become proficient due to peer assessment. Share the *Formative Strategies* with those students who have a learning gap in this area. Direct those students select a new strategy, practice that strategy with random topics over several class periods, and then are reassessed using the original topic.

Extension

Next, Student 2 works with Student 1 to tell a collective story. Student 1 says the first sentence then Student 2 says the second. They continue in this manner to continue the story. In addition, Student 2 asks questions or reacts as Student 1 tells the story. As a variation, Student 2 comes up with his/her own version of the story to tell about the same visual information and then the students compare their stories.

FIGURE 3.11 Narration/Storytelling Based on Pictures Assessment Form

Assessment: _____ *Date:* _____

	Student 1	*Student 2*
Topic		
Number: **Five-Frame Picture** *OR* *Number:* **One Picture**		
Improve		
New strategy		
Practice topics		
Reassess		
Number (original topic)		

FIGURE 3.12 Storytelling: Five-Frame Story

Formative Strategies for Narration/ Storytelling Based on Pictures

For the five-frame story, look for the turning point in the story in the fourth frame. Then go back and tell the beginning of the story (the introduction), the build up of the story, the turning point, and what finally happens (resolution).

For the five-frame story, describe the actions in each of the frames. Decide when you are describing a past situation, a present one, or future one. Use verbs in the appropriate tense. Practice using these tenses for another five-frame picture.

Think of all the details (Who? What? Where? When? Why? How? Which?) you can add to each frame in a five-frame story. For example, if the story is about a classroom problem and the first frame shows a student in a math class, you can make up additional information by giving the student a name, describing her, telling what she is feeling about the class, etc. Say at least three detailed sentences about each frame.

For a five-frame story, think of using time words to connect one picture to the next. You can connect the sentences with words such as "in the morning," "in the beginning," "then," "afterward," and "a few hours later."

Work with a peer who wants to improve in talking about a five-frame story. Each of you draws a different five-frame story. Both you and your partner describe the first story. Compare your information and reactions so that you have more to say about each frame. Then, do the same for the other five-frame story.

Go to Flickr (flickr.com) and type in any topic in your target language, such as *ville* (city in French). Print out five pictures that give you information about the city. Practice making up a story about the pictures.

For a five-frame picture, think of all the actions that are in each picture. Describe them in expanded sentences such as "They sit outside . . . The man talks to the women."

Look over a single picture, going from left to right and top to bottom as you would when reading, and tell a story as you go. Incorporate the objects or people in the picture into your story as you move across and down the picture. For example, "The woman is waiting for the train. She wears a winter coat because it is snowing. She sits on a chair. She is tired of waiting for the train. Next to her, another woman . . . " Try this with a picture from Flickr or Google Images, a picture you brought in, or a picture your teacher has. As a variation, imagine a three by three grid over the picture and describe each cell individually.

Make up a list of question words, such as *who, what, where, when, why, how, when*, and write them on a sheet of paper. Whenever you look at a picture, put your sheet next to it and answer each question for that picture. Expand on each answer. For example, for *who*, you might say "There is a man in the picture. He cooks. He has white clothing." Have a partner verify that you answer each question word for the picture.

Analyze a single picture, looking for its depicted event, its message, or its tone (sad, proud, joyous, etc.). Tell what things in the picture help show that event, message, or tone. For example, "Bob has a party in his house. They dance excitedly. The music is very loud." Do this for a picture from Flickr or Google Images, a picture you brought in, or a picture your teacher has.

$\wp$

Looking at a single picture, describe what happened before the event in the picture and what will happen next. Look at the actions in the picture to help you.

$\wp$

Using a single picture, pretend to be a person in the picture and describe or react to what is happening. For example, for a picture about a party you might say, "This party is boring. I'm sitting on the couch and no one else is on the couch. No one is talking to me." Try this with a picture from Flickr or Google Images, a picture you brought in, or a picture your teacher has.

$\wp$

Look at a single picture and describe what is going wrong and what the consequences are. For example, "The waiter carries hot soup. He drops the soup on the woman. She . . . " Try this with a picture from Flickr or Google Images, a picture you brought in, or a picture your teacher has.

$\wp$

Tell what different people might say about a single picture or how they would react to it. For example, describe the possible responses of these people: a grandparent or a senior citizen; another teenager; a parent; a business person; or an exchange student. As you think from each of their perspectives, find new things to say about the picture. Try this with a picture from Flickr or Google Images, a picture you brought in, or a picture your teacher has.

$\wp$

Think of someone famous (real, TV/movie, or book) or someone you know who has done something with the given topic. For example, for the topic of *travel*, you might think of a travel TV show you watch, such as "Anthony Bourdain: No Reservations." As you look at a five-frame picture that has people eating in an outside restaurant think of Bourdain eating in outside restaurants as he travels. Say what he says and does in these restaurants.

$\wp$

Pretend you are a sports announcer who tells everything that is happening during a game such as "He gets the brown ball. He quickly runs down the court. He looks around. He throws it to John. John makes three points." You can be a sports announcer for any event or situation in a picture. Practice this detailed announcing with any picture or any five-frame story. Look at the first frame and start saying details about it before moving on to the next frame.

$\wp$

Other strategy suggested by the teacher or peers:

Information and Opinion Functions

Purpose: To give as much information and opinions about a topic as possible within a minute
Level: Intermediate
Speaking Type: Presentational
Grouping: Groups of two
Form: Figure 3.13 Information and Opinion Functions Assessment Form (page 92)

Full Procedure

Explain to the students that Student 1 will start by giving as much information and opinions (likes, dislikes, and reasons) about the topic as possible in one minute. For example, "I eat in Bob's Burgers (information). I like their hamburgers (opinion); they are big (reason) . . . "

After you tell Student 1 the first topic (see the listing after the form) and say "Start," Student 1 gives information and then express his/her preferences. Students will use specific information and then give three additional statements to support their opinions about the information. Student 1 will have a minute and a half to give information and his/her opinion. Student 2 listens and records each information or opinion sentence with a slash. If Student 2 does not understand the statement or does not think that it expresses information or an opinion, he/she does not record a slash. At the end of a minute and a half, Student 2 will tally the slashes, record the number total, and report this information to Student 1. For half a minute, Student 2 offers other statements Student 1 could have used. Student 1 writes each suggestion in the "Improve" section of the form.

Next, the students roles. At the end of a minute and a half, Student 1 will tally the slashes, record the number total, and report this information to Student 2. For half a minute, Student 1 offers any statements that Student 1 could have used. Student 1 writes each suggestion in the "Improve" section of the form.

Implementing Formative Feedback

After you collect this assessment form, monitor each student's baseline. Scan the papers to identify those students who were already proficient according to your predetermined criteria or have become proficient due to peer assessment. Share the *Formative Strategies* with those students who have a learning gap in this area. Those students select a new strategy, practice that strategy with random topics over several class periods, and then are reassessed using the original topic.

Extension

Next, Student 2 immediately responds to each of Student 1's opinions by expressing his/her own opinion and giving reasons. Also, Student 2 can purposely disagree with each of Student 1's opinions. As an additional activity, Student 1 and Student 2 can act as "critics" who give their views on the same thing, such as a restaurant or a party.

Speaking Topics
First topics: react to a movie or TV show, comment on the weather
Second topics: complain about school, summarize your experiences at a local restaurant
Third topics: weekend activities, future job

Formative Strategies for Information and Opinion Functions

Information

Answer the five Ws (*who, what, where, when,* and *why*) plus *which, how,* and *how many* to give information about a given topic. For example, for the topic of *restaurant*, mentally ask yourself, "Who goes to the restaurant?" Say the answer, "My family goes to the restaurant," and then give an opinion about it: "My sister does not like the salad."

Describe the topic/situation to another person by including as many details as possible. Try for at least one detail per sentence, such as "My favorite store has a big sale on Friday."

See the "Detailed Information" assessment (page 61) for more information strategies.

Opinion

Look at a list of opinion/preference words, such as *like, do not like, really like,* and *hate,* from your notes, handouts, textbook, or a website. In any order, use each opinion word for some aspect of the given topic. For example, for a *restaurant* topic, you might say "I really like the hamburgers. They taste good." Speak on the topic of *your favorite restaurant*.

Make a list of the preference words from one extreme to another, such as *love, really like, like, do not like, hate,* and then say a sentence using each word/phrase about the given topic. Give a reason to support your opinion. For example, "I love the salads at Rob's Restaurant; they have a lot of chicken.

FIGURE 3.13 Information and Opinion Functions Assessment Form

Assessment: _____ Date: _____

	Student 1	Student 2
Topic		
Number: Information		
Number: Opinions		
Improve		
New strategy		
Practice topics		
Reassess		
Number (original topic)		

I really like their burritos with all the meat. I like their tacos with the thin shell." Practice by telling your preferences for *the classes you are taking*.

$\bigcirc$

Use expressions like "In my opinion," "I think," "I prefer," and "It seems to me" to express your opinion. Practice using each of these expressions with a topic such as *eating in the school cafeteria* with sentences such as "In my opinion, the food is wonderful."

$\bigcirc$

Look at a list of interjections that express your opinion, such as "How wonderful!" "How horrible!" "What a great game!" or "Great!" Then, without looking at the list, have your partner say five things about *your school team*. Respond with an appropriate interjection and a reason. For example, if your partner says, "Our team will win this game," you could respond with, "Impossible! John is sick."

$\bigcirc$

Think of contrasting nouns, verbs, adjectives, and adverbs to express your preference for the topic of *which mall you prefer to go to*. For example, using the contrasting adjectives *expensive/inexpensive* and *unpleasant/friendly*, you can say, "I like the inexpensive stores, not the expensive ones," and, "In Vizmart, the clerks are not pleasant, while in Betty's Boutique the clerks are friendly." Talk about your mall choice.

$\bigcirc$

Review phrases that express agreement or disagreement, such as "Me too!" "I agree" "Me neither" or "I don't agree." Work with a partner. As he/she says a sentence, respond with an agreement or a disagreement. For example, if he/she says, "The coach is horrible," you could respond, "I agree." Speak about the topic of *TV shows*.

$\bigcirc$

Add *because* to each statement to give a reason for your preference. For example, you might say, "I really like the pizza because it has plenty of cheese," or, "The pizza is good because it is big." Add an explanation to each preference. Give at least four reasons for each opinion: "I like it because . . . and because . . . and because . . . " Practice using preference statements by talking about *your favorite store* and why you like it.

$\bigcirc$

If several students want to improve in the area of information and opinion, have the group make a list of famous people or products, such as Justin Bieber or McDonalds. As each person or product is said, each person moves to the location in the room that represents how he/she feels about it, front of the room (really liking) to the back (hating). Afterwards, each student takes a turn sharing his/her feelings and gives two reasons why to the nearest person. Repeat this activity with ten different topics.

$\bigcirc$

Find two pictures for the given topic, such as pictures of two different cars you might buy, and tell which you prefer (your opinion) and why. Use the visual information to help you generate more reasons. You can bring in pictures, print out pictures from Flickr or Google Images, or use teacher-provided pictures.

Work with another student who wants to improve in the area of information and opinion. Have him/her say six common topics, such as six different sports. Respond to each of the six topics by saying a different opinion about each topic for 1) yourself, 2) a family member, and 3) a friend. Feel free to add additional information. For example, if your partner says, "Baseball," you could respond, "I do not like baseball. My father likes it; he watches each game. My friend, Maria, really likes baseball. She plays on two different teams." After your partner has said six topics and you have responded to each with an opinion, reverse roles.

Get together with three or four other students who want to improve in the area of information and opinion. Pick a topic, such as *my favorite restaurant*. Each student takes a turn saying what his/her favorite restaurant is and two reasons why. The other students respond by giving their opinions about the same restaurant and why they feel the way they do. Think of the reasons others used and incorporate those reasons to support your own opinions.

Other strategy suggested by the teacher or peers:

Explanations with *Because* and Other Complex Sentences

Purpose: To explain the reason for something with as many "complex" sentences as possible. (Although a complex sentence is technically one with an independent and a dependent clause and words like *because, since, after, although,* and *when,* the term will be used here in a general sense to also include sentences with two independent clauses that are connected with words such as *but, yet,* and *and.*)

Level: Intermediate

Speaking Type: Presentational

Grouping: Groups of two

Form: Figure 3.14 Explanations with *Because* and Other Complex Sentences Assessment Form (page 97)

Full Procedure

Explain to the students that Student 1 will start by saying as many complex reasons as possible using *because, but, when* etc. about the given topic in one minute. For example, "My brother, Pablo, plays well because he runs fast" or "When my sister throws well, her team wins."

After you tell Student 1 the first topic (see the listing after the form) and say "Start," he/she makes up complex sentences about it for one minute. Student 2 writes a slash for every sentence that has *because/but* or similar words under Student 1. Student 2 listens. If Student 2 does not understand the sentence, he/she does not record any information. At the end of the minute, Student 2 tallies the response, writes down the number total and reports back to Student 1. Then, for half a minute Student 2 goes over any sentence that did not seem complex and helps Student 1 make that sentence and any others more complex. These new sentences are written in the "Improve" section of the form.

Next, the students reverse roles, with Student 2 doing the speaking for the new topic. At the end of the minute, Student 1 tallies the response, writes down the number total and reports back to Student 2. Then, for half a minute Student 1 goes over any sentence that did not seem complex and helps Student 2 make that sentence and any others more complex.

Implementing Formative Feedback

After you collect the assessment form, monitor each student's baseline. Scan the papers to identify those students who were already proficient according to your predetermined criteria or have become proficient due to peer assessment. Share the *Formative Strategies* with those students who have a learning gap in this area. Those students select a new strategy, practice that strategy with random topics over several class periods, and then are reassessed using the original topic.

Extension

Next, the students can redo this assessment by having their partners respond to each of their statements by giving a reaction, agreeing, disagreeing, and giving reasons in complex sentences. Students can tell the ten top reasons for a topic, such as *why Duke is the best basketball team* or *why Carrie Underwood is the best singer*.

Speaking Topics
First topics: contrast two restaurants/stores; tell which athlete, singer, or actor you prefer and why

Second topics: contrast two different places or cities; tell which of these you prefer and why: an old cell phone and a new one, a new video game system and an old one, and an old computer and a new one

Third topics: household chores, town/neighborhood

Formative Strategies for Explanations with *Because* and Other Complex Sentences

Review comparatives, such as *tall/taller/tallest*, and comparison phrasing, such as "is taller than," from your notes, textbook, or a website. Use the comparison strategy to talk about *two friends*. You might say, "Ana is smarter than Juana because Ana studies. Juana is a better athlete because she practices."

$\bigcirc$

Pick two people or objects and say as many contrasting statements in complex sentences as possible by using the contrasting adjectives. For example, for the topic of *different friends*, you can use the adjective pairs of *short/tall* in a sentence like "Raquel is short but Huan is tall."

$\bigcirc$

For the topic of *family*, use verbs that show a contrast in the complex sentences. For example, "Rowan works for four hours while Lily sleeps for four hours" or "Jane picks up her clothing but John puts his clothing on the floor."

$\bigcirc$

As soon as you have your topic, pick two very famous or familiar people, objects, etc. that you know very much about and that have many differences. For example, for the topic of *restaurant*, think of all the major differences between your favorite restaurant and your least favorite restaurant. Do a mental graphic organizer to go through the major differences with such topics

FIGURE 3.14 Explanations with *Because* and Other Complex Sentences Assessment Form

Assessment: _____ Date: _____

	Student 1	Student 2
Topic		
Number: complex sentences with reasons		
Improve		
New strategy		
Practice topics		
Reassess		
Number (original topic)		

as *types of food*, *taste of food*, and *amount of food*. For example, you may say, "Rick's Restaurant serves a big salad but Doris' Diner serves a small salad."

You and your partner individually write out ten short sentences for a topic such as *the weekend*. Write each sentence on a slip of paper. Then mix up the sentences, select any two, and see if you can make them into a one complex sentence about the topic. If you cannot, discard one sentence and pick up another one. Your partner checks that you have a meaningful complex sentence. Next your partner does the same. Continue until you have made complex sentences of all the original sentences. Read through your sentences once more. Then, make up a conversation about the topic loosely based on the complex sentences you just said.

For the topic of *my favorite TV show*, your partner says two simple sentences and you connect them into one complex sentence. Then say two simple sentences that your partner makes in to a complex sentence. Next, converse about the topic using complex sentences.

Complex words help you to explain your ideas in depth. Each category of complex words for dependent clauses serves a different purpose:

- Sequence: before, while, after, when, whenever, until
- Cause and effect: because, since, unless, whether, unless, if
- Contrast: but, although, even though

For the topic of *the mall*, you may say "Before I go to the mall, I make a list of what I need" or "Because the store has sales, I buy many things." Practice saying a sentence for each complex word for the topic of *the city*.

For a topic, use time references to help create complex sentences. For the topic of *your school classes*, tell what you do today, add *but*, and tell what you will do differently tomorrow. For example, "Today I study history for thirty minutes, but tomorrow I will study history for one hour." You can also use *today* and *tomorrow*, such as what you do today and what you did yesterday with the topic. For example, "Today in English I read a story, but yesterday I wrote a composition." Make sure to include complete information in each sentence and not just the verb.

Say multiple reasons to support your views about a topic such as *why your city is a great city*. Use different complex words. For example, you may say, "My city is great 1) because . . . 2) since . . . 3) when . . . 4) due to . . . 5) so . . . "

Ask six questions using complex questions to find out information about a topic such as *class*. For example, you might ask, "What did you do before you came to class?" or "How will you do on the test since you only studied for five minutes?" Your partner answers and then asks you six questions using complex sentences about an exam.

$\wp$

Review the strategies in the "Information and Opinions Functions" section (page 90). Then use these to say complex ideas about your favorite vacation spot.

$\wp$

Other strategy suggested by the teacher or peers:

Directions/Commands

Purpose: To be able to say as many directions or commands about a topic in a minute

Level: Intermediate

Speaking Type: Presentational

Grouping: Groups of two

Form: Standard Speaking Assessment Form

Full Procedure

Explain to the students that Student 1will say as many full directions as possible about a task topic, such as *telling a friend how to dance like Lady Gaga,* for one minute. Think of what you will normally tell a person to do. Each command should be more than just the verb. For example, "Walk!" could be changed to "Walk to the store." "Put" can become "Do not put the book on the desk."

After you tell Student 1 the first topic (see the listing after the Form) and say "Start," Student 1 says commands for the given topic. Student 2 only marks complete directions, not phrases such as "Stop!" or "Sing!" At the end of a minute, Student 2 tells Student 1 the number of commands said, any major mistakes in the commands, the correct form for any incorrect commands, or what else Student 1 could have said. These are recorded in the "Improve" section of the form. Then, as the teacher gives a different topic to Student 2 and says, "Start," the students reverse roles. The students look over the suggestions for improvements, practice using them, and reassess themselves using the additional reassessment topics.

Implementing Formative Feedback

After you collect this assessment form, monitor each student's baseline. Scan the papers to identify those students who were already proficient according to your predetermined criteria or have become proficient due to peer assessment. Share the *Formative Strategies* with those students who have a learning gap in this area. Those students select a new strategy, practice that strategy with random topics over several class periods, and then are reassessed using the original topic.

Extension

Next, Student 1 can rearrange the directions so that they demonstrate a logical sequence one would find in real life, such as a how-to manual. As a variation, Student 2 can perform the commands as Student 1 says them. Likewise, Student 2 can draw the commands in stick figures. In addition, Student 2 can ask Student 1 questions about each command. If Student 1 says, "Walk to the store," Student 2 can ask "Which store?" or "How far is it to the store?"

Speaking Topics
First topics: say commands to your younger brother or sister while you babysit him/her for the evening, help your friend decide which cell phone to buy

Second topics: tell your sports team what it can do to improve during a game and tell the other team what to do, command your pet

Third topics: getting and preparing food, walking to a city location

Formative Strategies for Directions/Commands

Review a grammar form from your textbook, a handout or an online grammar presentation that explains how to change a verb to the command form. The online grammar presentation can be found by searching for language +commands +PowerPoint such as Chinese +commands +PowerPoint. Look carefully for any differences in giving commands, such as to one or several people, giving commands to people you know and people you do not know, and giving positive or negative commands. Practice commands in an online program such as Quia. Then use those verbs to say full sentence commands to your partner such as those your teacher says to you during the class.

Find a list of common infinitives such as those at the end of your textbook chapter. Make them into directions for one of the chapter's topics. For example, for the chapter topic of *house*, use the infinitive to help you say the directions your parents would say to you, such as "Pick up your clothes" and "Clean your room." After you say each direction, have a partner check its form and meaning. Then your partner does directions for another textbook topic such as *things to do outside your house*.

Practice commands with another student who wants to improve in the area of giving directions. Make up a list of many infinitives about a given topic such as *cooking your favorite meal*. Give at least eight commands for this topic. Your partner verifies that each command is in the correct form and that your commands include all the necessary steps to do the task. Then, the partner selects a topic, writes up a list of infinitives for it, and then says the commands while you check on his/her commands and the completeness of the commands.

With a partner, pick two common topics to say directions about, such as directions that your work boss would say to the workers in your department or directions that a tour guide uses as he/she gives a tour of your city. For each topic, each of you should think of directions. Your partner listens to your directions for the topic and makes any needed corrections. Then you listen to your partner's directions and help him/her. Next, identify which different directions you each used so that each of you can add more directions to the topic.

Play "Simon Says" using classroom commands with a partner or a small group. One of you says the commands, such as Simon Says, "Sit down in the chair," while the others listen to see if the commands are said correctly and then quickly and correctly perform the actions. For example, Simon Says can be played with daily classroom actions, such as "Go to the chalk board" or with sport actions such as "Get the ball." Each person does a series for his/her commands topic.

Think about and say directions for a topic such as *how to be an A student, how to take care of a pet*, or *how to make a certain food*. Your partner can verify that you use the correct directions and that your directions will lead to the desired end. You can "edit" your directions so that others can listen and perform the task. You can digitally record these oral directions by using a microphone and a computer program like Audacity or Voki. Then listen to your partners' directions and give him/her feedback.

Play "robot." Your partner is a robot who can only do exactly what you command in a step-by-step method. Have him/her do a task such as *put the book on the teacher's desk* by giving him/her all the necessary sub commands such as "Stand up" and "Pick up the book." Your robot partner raises his/her hand if you have missed a step such as "Walk to the desk" or have said a command incorrectly. Do for *throw away a piece of paper* or *draw a circle on the board*.

Work in a group of three to four. Each person creates a commercial to sell something from his/her house, such as a lamp. Each student can bring in the object or a picture of it. Each seller will give his/her listeners at least eight commands such as "Look at this lamp. Notice its interesting color . . . " After the group listens to an individual, they will correct any commands that were done incorrectly, were not in the appropriate order, or did not convey enough meaning. You will make changes to your selling commands and re-give your sales pitch.

Think of a childhood game and orally tell the directions for playing that game. If possible, bring that game to class. Have your partner check if he/she feels that he/she can play the game. Then reverse roles with the partner, who will tell you how to play a game.

Pick something in your target language's culture to give commands about, such as *protecting the environment, preserving folk music,* or *going to the farmers' markets instead of big box grocery stores.* Find pictures of the cultural area on Flickr or Google Images and then give commands to the people of the country about this culture. Your partner will check that you use meaningful verbs and the appropriate command form of those verbs.

Other strategy suggested by the teacher or peers:

Information and Persuasion Functions

Purpose: To say as much information and as many persuasion statements as possible within a minute for a given topic
Level: Intermediate
Speaking Type: Presentational
Grouping: Groups of two
Form: Figure 3.15 Information and Persuasion Functions Assessment Form) page 106)

Full Procedure
Explain to the students that Student 1 will start by giving information and by trying to persuade the partner about the topic in one minute. For example, "Bob's Burgers is a great restaurant. The meat in their MegaBurger is delicious. Their French Fries are spicy. You should go to Bob's Burgers."

After you tell Student 1 the first topic (see the listing after the form) and say "Start," Student 1 gives information and then tries to persuade Student 2 to do something. Student 1 will provide additional statements to support his/her persuasion. Student 1 will have a minute and a half to give information and persuade his/her partner. Student 2 listens and records each function sentence with a slash if each sentence is comprehensible and either gives information or persuades. At the end of a minute and a half, Student 2 tallies the slashes, writes down the number total and reports back to Student 1. As Student 2 indicates what other information or preference Student 1 could have used, Student 1 writes down each suggestion in the "Improve" section of the form. Then they reverse roles for the next topic. They look over the suggestions and practice. Then they redo these topics.

Implementing Formative Feedback
After you collect this assessment form, monitor each student's baseline. Scan the papers to identify those students who were already proficient according to your predetermined criteria or have become proficient due to peer assessment. Share the *Formative Strategies* with those students who have a learning gap in this area. Those students select a new strategy, practice that strategy with random topics over several class periods, and then are reassessed using the original topic.

Extension
Next, the students can change the assessment so that Student 2 responds after each information or persuasion statement. Also, they can change this into an

argument where the Student 2 disagrees with the information and persuasion statements; Student 2 listens to Student 1 and then begins the disagreement. They can ask a third student to decide who gives the most convincing arguments.

Speaking Topics—Convince your partner to or not to:
First topics: go to a beach/a lake, stay out late on a school night
Second topics: go to a faraway mall, store, or place; study for a big test with you
Third topics: help you with your work, play a certain sport

Formative Strategies for Information and Persuasion Functions

Information

Answer the five Ws (*who, what, where, when,* and *why*) plus *which, how* and *how many* to give information about the topic, such as *a great restaurant*. For example, mentally ask yourself, "Who goes to the restaurant?" and say the answer, "My family goes to the restaurant." Then give an opinion about it: "My sister does not like the salad."

Describe the topic/situation to another person by including as many details as possible. Try for at least one detail per sentence, such as "On Saturday I wake up at 10 o'clock. I shower for twenty minutes."

See "Detailed Information Sentences About a Topic" (page 61) for more information strategies.

Persuasion

Review all of the persuasion function words, such as expressing an opinion (*I think that, It seems to me*), alternative action (*What do think of . . . ? Would you like to . . . ?*), and asking for agreement (*Do you like the idea of . . . ? This is helpful, isn't it?*), from your notes, handouts, the textbook, or a web page. Use each persuasion expression in a sentence about a topic, such as *talking someone into going to a specific restaurant*. For example, "Mary says the new restaurant is good. It has great steaks. They have many desserts. What do you think of going there?"

Review contrasting adjectives, nouns, and verbs and then use these contrasts to convince your partner to go to a certain movie or for him/her to convince

FIGURE 3.15 Information and Persuasion Functions Assessment Form

Assessment: _____ *Date:* _____

	Student 1	*Student 2*
Topic		
Number: Information		
Number: Persuasion		
Improve		
New strategy		
Practice topics		
Reassess		
Number (original topic)		

you to go to the movies on a certain night. For example, you might contrast two movies by saying, "In the first movie the weak men sit in an office, while, in the second movie the strong men fight in the countryside." Your partner will count the number of sentences with contrasting words.

Use comparisons to help you convince your partner *which store is better*. You can say phrases such as "My store is bigger than your store. My store has more clothing than your store." Pick two stores and persuade your partner about which is better by using comparisons. Your partner will keep track of the number of comparisons you use.

Use quantity adjectives, such as *more, many, less,* and *little,* as you show that your idea or object is better than another. For example, you can try to persuade your partner that your ideal car is better than another with a statement such as "My car gets more miles per gallon. It uses less gasoline." Think of other possible persuasion statements using quantity adjectives about the topic of *cars*.

After you say one sentence of basic information about the given topic, say at least four reasons to convince your partner before you suggest he/she do it your way. Practice this formula of 1-4-1 (1 information sentence, 4 reasons, 1 invitation or request) by persuading your partner to drink a certain soft drink. Your partner can practice persuading you to eat a certain cereal.

Think of several commercials you have seen on TV and how they persuade you. Pick one that you thought was very persuasive. Do a mini-version of that commercial in your target language.

Think about how your partner will benefit by doing the thing you want him/her to do. What are the advantages of following your preference? Why will it appeal to him/her? For example, imagine you are trying to sell a backpack to a classmate. Why should a classmate want that backpack? Say all the advantages of the backpack.

Work with another student who wants to improve in the area of information and persuasion. Pick a topic (for example, *all students should wear uniforms to school*) and then each of you pick a side to argue (for or against). Think of all the sentences you can use to persuade the other person. Have a mini-debate. Each person gives information and then a reason (persuasion). After two minutes of debating, talk over all the persuasion techniques you used and what else you could have said to persuade the other person.

Create a quick multimedia presentation, such as pictures in PowerPoint for your key points in the argument about which college is better. Include pictures that help you to convince your partner. Present to your partner. Then have your partner react to your key points by saying something like "You said . . . but. . . . " Then, your partner does his/her presentation and you convince him/her that your point of view is better by using "You said . . . but. . . . "

Ask questions to help convince your partner. As your partner gives a reason, ask a question about the reason. For example, if your partner says, "I like the Ithaca Mall over the Lansing Mall because it has more stores," you can ask, "Does the Ithaca Mall have many sports stores?" since you know that it doesn't. You might ask other questions, such as "Why do you want to . . . ?" "How are you going to . . . ?" "What are your reasons for. . . . " and "What will happen when . . . ?" Convince your partner that your mall is better by asking him/her questions.

Use various propaganda techniques such as glittering generalities (vague words like "the best"), testimonials (famous people talking about or using the product), plain folk (symbols or words to show that normal folks do or use this), band wagon (everyone else is doing it), name calling (saying negative things), card stacking (omitting the negative about your item), and false analogy (two things are presented as being similar). For example, in order to persuade your partner that your cell phone is better than his/hers, say that the president uses the same cell phone you do (testimonial). Try to convince each other about which cell phone is better.

Other strategy suggested by the teacher or peers:

Explanation Through Alternative Actions

Purpose: To explain by giving alternative actions or suggestions for a situation
Level: Intermediate
Speaking Type: Interpersonal
Grouping: Groups of two
Form: Figure 3.16 Explanation Through Alternative Actions Assessment Form (page 111)

Full Procedure

Explain to the students that Student 1 and Student 2 will explain or give alternative suggestions or actions for a situation in as many sentences as possible in one minute. If your friend wants to go bowling and you do not want to, you suggest an alternative of playing baseball and explain your reasons.

Both students read the situation conversation starter and when you say "Start," Student 1 takes on the first role and then starts the conversation such as borrowing the family car for the weekend. Student 2 responds or asks a question; he or she takes on the role of a person with a different opinion than the first person. Try to say at least six utterances about the topic to resolve the issue or show the other person your viewpoint. Each utterance has to be a complete sentence; compound or complex sentences are preferred. Greetings like "Hi" and Leave taking like "See you tomorrow" statements do not count. Student 2 records each time Student 1 says something and Student 1 records for Student 2. At the end of a minute, they show each other their speaking score. They decide if Student 1 completed the task such as being able to borrow the family car. They think of what else Student 1 could have done to solve the situation.

They reverse roles with Student 2 starting the speaking for the new situation topic. At the end of a minute, they show each other their speaking score. They think of what else they can say about the situation.

Implementing Formative Feedback

After you collect this assessment form, monitor each student's baseline. Scan the papers to identify those students who were already proficient according to your predetermined criteria or have become proficient due to peer assessment. Share the *Formative Strategies* with those students who have a learning gap in this area. Those students select a new strategy, practice that strategy with random topics over several class periods and then are reassessed using the original topic.

Extension

You may extend the time for this conversation to three minutes. Your students can create their own situations based on real situations in their school, job, sports/hobbies, relationships and family. They can do a Point/Counterpoint type of conversation in which Student 1 gives one viewpoint while Student 2 suggests an alternative way of viewing it.

Speaking Topics
First topics
Situation 1: You and your friends want to go to the movies. You disagree with your friend's movie choice and explain to your friend the advantages of your movie choice. You start.

Situation 2: You do not get home until 1:00 a.m. on a school night. Your father is upset since he has not heard from you and you usually get home from work at 9:00 p.m. Your partner is your father/mother. You start.

Second topics
Situation 1: You arrive at your hotel but the hotel does not have you as a guest. Student 1 = you, Student 2 = hotel employee. You start.

Situation 3: Your friend is upset because you did not do anything for his/her birthday. Student 1 = you; Student 2 = friend. You start.

Third topics
Situation 1: A friend wants to borrow fifty dollars. Student 1 = you, Student 2 = the friend.

Situation 2: Your parents want you to do chores but you want to go out with friends. Student 1 = you, Student 2 = parents.

Formative Strategies for Explanation Through Alternative Actions

Listen to the situation to figure out what the real problem is and how to solve it. Summarize the problem in a few critical words. For the situation, "You and your friends want to go to the movies. You disagree with your friend's choice of movies and you suggest the alternative of your friend going to your movie," you reduce it down to "explain to my friend whey he/she should go to my movie." Then you think of sentences to express ways of convincing. Do this topic with your partner.

If you do not know a word, use a more general word (use "meat" if you cannot remember "steak" and use "clothing" for the specific "shirt") or another

FIGURE 3.16 Explanation Through Alternative Actions Assessment Form

Assessment: _____ Date: _____

	Student 1	Student 2
Topic		
Number: Questions		
Number: Statements		
Improve		
New strategy		
Practice topics		
Reassess		
Number (original topic)		

word that expresses a similar action (say "walk" when you cannot remember "run"; say "eat" if you cannot remember "chew"). As your partner talks about the topic of *why she did not do the homework* to a teacher, you paraphrase each sentence to use different words for the same idea.

Think of this situation as a debate. Explain your actions/ideas with *because* or similar-type statements. Your goal is to have more points (positive statements on your side) than your partner. Think, "I am right because. . . ." and come up with as many *because* statements as you can. Practice using the topic of *arguing with an exchange student about whose school is better*.

One way to solve a situation is by asking questions of the other person. When the person says something such as "I'm mad at you," you can ask "Why are you mad at me?" When the person answers, ask another question to learn more about the real problem. For example, the person answers, "I'm mad because we had a date tonight" and you ask, "When was the date?" Pick a situation such as a teacher (your partner) telling a student (you) that he/she is failing and the student asks questions to find out why.

Often situations are resolved by showing sympathy or consideration for the other person. Review how to say phrases like "I'm sorry," "I did not know," "Are you OK now?" "I would like to help you . . . " and "What can we do to . . . " Think of a problem topic such as *a friend who has to miss a party because his/her parents are sick* and think of all the sympathy or consideration statements you can say (the friend can be played by your partner).

Focus in on a specific time when you, a friend, or TV or movie character was in the situation of trying to talk someone out of doing something dangerous, such as driving a car without using lights, playing in an old abandoned building, or diving into a lake with hidden rocks. Use that information in this situation. Practice with another student who role plays considering one of the previous situations while you talk him/her out of it. Then you role play doing one of the other previous situations while your partner talks you out of it.

Before you start speaking, mentally brainstorm critical words and commonly used sentences for the situation and use those in the situation. For example, for the situation topic of *deciding where to eat before going to a movie*, mentally review food words and phrases. Talk through this eating before movie situation with a partner.

Identify the problem and then think of what advice your parents or friends would give you. Use their ideas. For example, what would your best friend, your parent, your brother/sister, or your grandparent tell you about how to break up with your boyfriend/girlfriend? Do this situation with a partner. Then switch roles. Your partner has to resolve this differently. Compare how each of you solved the problem.

Work with another person who wants to improve in the area of explanations. Each of you will brainstorm individually and then share all the typical statements or questions people will say in the situation of an exchange student who lives with you wanting to go shopping on the day before your big test. Help each other to respond to the statements or questions. Then talk your way through this situation.

Use a problem solving approach of identifying the problem, thinking of possible solutions, brainstorming the advantages and disadvantages of each solution, and then selecting the best solution from the choices. Go through these steps as you and a partner decide how to celebrate your first day of summer vacation.

Other strategy suggested by the teacher or peers:

Description of Past, Present, and Future Events in the Same Conversation

Purpose: To say as many sentences describing past, present, and future events

Level: Advanced

Speaking Type: Presentational

Grouping: Groups of two

Form: Figure 3.17 Description of Past, Present, and Future Events in the Same Conversation Assessment Form

Full Procedure

Explain to the students that Student 1 will start by speaking about the same topic for past, present, and future events in as many sentences as possible in one minute. For example, the student can talk about all the things he/she did last night to get ready for school today, the various things he/she does today in school, and the many activities he/she will do in school tomorrow.

After you tell Student 1 the first topic (see the listing after the form) and say "Start," he/she talks about it for a minute and a half using past, present, and future tenses. Student 2 listens and makes a slash for each time each tense is used; if Student 2 is not sure of the tense or does not understand the tense, he/she does not record a slash. At the end of the time, Student 2 records the slashes as a number and reports back to Student 1 how many present, past, and future verbs he/she used.

Next, the students reverse roles. After Student 1 tallies the slashes, writes down the total, and reports back to Student 2, they both think of ways to use the tenses correctly and to organize their thinking so that they can use the three tenses for the same topic. They write these in the "Improve" section of the form. Then they practice with a random topic from their textbook and reassess.

Implementing Formative Feedback

After you collect this assessment form, monitor each student's baseline. Scan the papers to identify those students who were already proficient according to your predetermined criteria or have become proficient due to peer assessment. Share the *Formative Strategies* with those students who have a learning gap in this area. Those students select a new strategy, practice that strategy with random topics over several class periods, and are then reassessed using the original topic.

FIGURE 3.17 Description of Past, Present, and Future Events in the Same Conversation Assessment Form

Assessment: _____ Date: _____

	Student 1	Student 2
Topic		
Number: Past		
Number: Present		
Number: Future		
Improve		
New strategy		
Practice topics		
Reassess		
Number (original topic)		

Extension

Next, Student 1 speaks again on the same topic by telling a story about an event. Student 2 can ask questions, request clarification, or react while Student 1 speaks. The students can also take turns talking about the same event and comparing their experiences. Try doing an oral documentary about an event: what has led up to now, what is happening now, and what will happen in the future.

Speaking Topics
First topics: a trip, a store
Second topics: sports, a party
Third topics: a class test, a meal

Formative Strategies for Description of Past, Present, and Future Events in the Same Conversation

Make a three column form for Past, Present, and Future and then list past, present, and future actions for a topic, such as *your father's or mother's life*. Tell what the parent used to, does now, and wants to do in the future. Say several sentences for each column (Figure 3.18).

Make a list of many time words for the past, present, and future. For example, for the past you may list words like "yesterday," "last week," "last year," and "in 2005." Sometimes when you use different time words, you can more easily organize your thinking about what was, what is, and what will be. For example, you may find it easier to talk about past, present, and future actions when you use the different terms *before*, *now*, and *tomorrow*. Find out which time words work for you in the target language. Use them to talk about the topic of *food*.

FIGURE 3.18 Verb Tense Columns

Past	Present	Future

Make a grammar verb "help sheet" in which you summarize common verbs in the past, present, and future forms. If you temporarily forget a tense, you can use this help sheet. As you encounter other important or irregular verbs, write these down in the appropriate place on the sheet. Practice talking about vacations: what your last vacation was like, what this year's one is like, and what you want to do on your next vacation.

Think of describing the differences between past, present, and future events by using the same verb for each time period. For example, you may say, "Yesterday I studied an hour for math (tell more about yesterday's studying). . . . Today I study for thirty minutes for English (tell more about today's studying). . . . Tomorrow, Saturday, I will not study (tell more about what you will do instead of studying)." Notice that each different phrase uses the same verb, "to study." Practice by describing the different actions you can take in the past, present, and future for the topic of *your family's daily actions*.

Practice the tenses by going through your visual verb flashcards (picture on one side, target language on the other). After you see the first four cards, use the verbs to describe what you did yesterday. Then use the next four cards to describe what you are doing today. Use the last four cards to describe what you will do tomorrow.

Take your first ten visual verb flashcards (picture on one side, target language on the other), look at the picture drawings, and quickly arrange them in a logical sequence. Then use that order to tell about the past, then the present, and then the future. Say the first three verbs in the past, the next four in the present, and the remaining three in the future.

Tell a personal story about being with friends. Think of what you did to get ready, what you are doing today, and what you will do in the future. For example, "Yesterday Chris invited me to a party [Tell what you did to get ready for the party]. . . . Today, at the party I dance with Carla [Tell more about dancing or the actual party]. . . . Tomorrow we'll have lunch at the mall [Tell more about what will happen at lunch or afterward]."

Think of the logical steps in doing something such as a vacation. Think of making "to-do lists" for the past, the present, and the future aspects of the vacation. What did you do to get ready for it? What are you doing on your vacation? What type vacation will you take next time? Talk about the topic of *vacation* using a past, present, and future narration.

Retell a story from a TV show, movie, or book series. Tell what happened up to now, what the character is doing now, and what future or alternative actions he/she will take. For example, you could talk about *Twilight* books or movies.

💬

Think of the given topic in the context of your autobiography. Personalize it. Tell about your past ("When I was a child, I. . . . "), your present ("As a teenager, I now. . . . "), and your future ("As an adult, I will. . . . "). Talk with your partner in three tenses about the topic of *family*.

💬

Talk about your *wants* for certain objects over time. You can tell about the things you used to want, the things you want now, and the things you will want in the future. As a variation, talk about gifts that you received as a child, gifts you receive now, and gifts you will receive when you are 50.

💬

Talk about your given topic by focusing on big changes over time. For the topic of *school*, think about what schools used to be like in the far past, what they are like now, and what they will be like in the far future. Focus on the differences for each time period. For example, "In schools of the past, all students were in the same classroom. They wrote using chalk. . . . "

💬

Other strategy suggested by the teacher or peers:

Complex Narration Using Multiple Topics in the Same Conversation

Purpose: To use complex narration about multiple different topics in the same conversation

Level: Advanced

Speaking: Interpersonal

Grouping: Groups of two

Form: Figure 3.19 Complex Narration Using Multiple Topics in the Same Conversation Assessment Form (page 121)

Full Procedure

Explain to the students that Student 1 and Student 2 will talk together as much as possible about one topic, connect the first topic to a second topic, talk about the second topic and then connect the second topic to a third one. They will talk for two minutes. You can use the first topic in the subsequent topics or you can treat each topic individually. For example, if the topics are *animal*, *house*, and *clothing*, students could talk about an animal, what that animal does in the house, and what clothing it wears or plays with. Or students could talk about an animal, connect that animal to a room in the house, then talk about rooms in the house (not the animal), connect the house to clothing, and, finally, talk about clothing (not animal or room). Students should give as much information as possible for each topic.

As you show the students the three topics to incorporate into one conversation, Student 1 writes down the topics on the form. After you say "Start," Student 1 asks or talks about the first topic to Student 2, who joins in talking about the first topic. Student 2 records how many sentences or questions are asked about the topic. Then they connect the first topic to the second one, talk about the second topic, connect it to the third topic, and talk about the third one. Student 2 again records the topic and the number of sentences or questions asked. Students will be given the three topics to incorporate.

When they finish this two-minute conversation, they think of how they can go more easily from one topic to another. Student 2 records each suggestion in the "Improve" section of the form. They look over these and re-do the topic.

Implementing Formative Feedback

After you collect this assessment form, monitor each student's baseline. Scan the papers to identify those students who were already proficient according to your predetermined criteria or have become proficient due to peer assessment. Share the *Formative Strategies* with those students who have a learning gap in this area. Those students select a new strategy, practice that strategy with random topics over several class periods, and then are reassessed using the original topic.

Extension

Ask students to listen to conversations in the hallway and cafeteria and then list the different topics that occur in normal conversations. Then ask them to use some of these topics in a conversation.

For a fun activity, students can also play "Speaking Hot Potato," a collaborative speaking exercise in which students try to link one topic to the next. To play, a group of students is given a pile of topic cards. The first student draws a card and says a sentence about the topic. The student to his/her left then draws a card and says a sentence connecting the first topic to the second. Then the next student draws a card, and so on.

Speaking Topics
First topics: family/sports/food, school/city/travel
Second topics: work/holidays/music, seasons/health/clothing
Third topics: house/health/park, hotel/celebration or holiday/bank

Formative Strategies for Complex Narration Using Multiple Topics in the Same Conversation

Think of approaching multiple topics either as linear connections or as jumping off points. In linear connections, the first item remains the focus, even when talking about the other two topics. For example, for *season/city/music*, you can talk about a season such as summer, what summer looks like in the city, and what music is played during the summer. On the other hand, if you use the three topics as different jumping-off points, you talk about a season, connect it to the city with one sentence, talk about the city (not dealing with the season), connect it with one sentence to music and talk about the music (not dealing with the season or city). The second approach resembles the random connections made in many conversations. Try each of the approaches for *season/city/music*.

As soon as you and your speaking partner have the three topics, make a quick mental list of some nouns and actions for each topic. For the topics of *clothing/house/celebration*, you might list "shirts, pants, tie, wear, put on" for the first topic. Say sentences about the first topic, connect it to the second, say sentences about the second, connect it to third, and then talk about the third. Use

FIGURE 3.19 Complex Narration Using Multiple Topics in the Same Conversation Assessment Form

Assessment: _____ Date: _____

	Student 1	Student 2
Topic		
Number: Topic 1		
Number: Topic 2		
Number: Topic 3		
Improve		
New strategy		
Practice topics		
Reassess		
Number (original topic)		

these topics with your partner, who will do the same for the topics of *weather/concert/restaurant*.

$\bigcirc$

With another person who wants to improve in the area of complex narration, play "Commonality Tag." Think of any two topics, such as *city* and *weather*; then brainstorm with your partner to think of all the sentences that you can use to connect the two topics. For the above two topics, you might say, "People go to the city's swimming pool, when it is hot" or "City people have trouble with snow in winter." Talk about the first topic for several sentences, add in one of the commonality tags, and then say sentences for the second topic. Play commonality tag for the topic pairs *family/education*, *house/leisure activities*, *shopping/community*, and *meals/travel*.

$\bigcirc$

Pick three topics and think of a personal story, real-life situation, TV show or movie, or a book that incorporates all three topics and retell the situation/story. For example, for the topics of *health/job/celebration* you could tell a story about breaking your arm in a skating accident, how that effected your job, and how you celebrated when your arm was healed.

$\bigcirc$

Think back to a conversation you had with a friend or family member. Think of how the conversation wandered from topic to topic. List all of the different topics that you covered during that one conversation. Perhaps, you started with *school*, then *work*, and next *buying a car*. With a partner, try to duplicate that conversation using three topics in the target language.

$\bigcirc$

You may find that you can improve in complex narration by mentally working backward from the last topic to the second and then to the first. For *clothing, house, celebration*, think of a celebration (the last topic), then what you do in your house to get ready for the celebration (the second topic), and then what clothing you buy or have to have for a celebration (the first topic). This thinking follows the pattern of "in order to do this, I need to do this." Work backward through *home, travel, music* and *sleep, class, hobby* and then describe the topics in their original order.

$\bigcirc$

With a partner, make fifteen 3 × 5 inch cards, each with a different topic written on it. Randomly pick three cards. You and your partner work together to say four sentences about the first card topic. You could each say two sentences or one of you can say three while the other says one. Then connect the first card topic to the second and say four more sentences. Next, connect the second topic to the third card topic and say four more sentences. Talk about what additional sentences you could say about each topic and how you can better connect one topic to another.

$\bigcirc$

As you talk about a topic, provide information that answers the five Ws (*who, what, where, when, why*). Keep asking and answering the question words until a question's answer connects from one topic to another. For example, for the topics of *eat, sport, house*, you might say, "I eat at Ron's Restaurant (Where?). I have two hamburgers (What?). My friend, Tom, (Who?) eats three hamburgers there (What?). Tom plays baseball with me (Who?)." Notice that the question "Who?" connected eating to sports (baseball). Try using questions to connect *eat, sport, house*.

Use time to connect the given topics, such as *mall, movie, house*. You can use time references such as hours (at 8:00, at 9:00, at 11:00), parts of the day (in the morning, in the afternoon, in the evening), and relative time terms (then, next, after, before). For example, you may say, "At ten o'clock we enter the mall (talk more about the mall). . . . At twelve o'clock we leave for the movie (talk more about leaving or the movie). . . . At two o'clock we go to Helena's house (talking about what you will do in her house)." Use time references as you connect the topics *animal/park/doctor* or *friend/party/sick*.

Play "Conversation Tag" with your partner using the given topics. Start talking about the first topic by saying two to three sentences about it; then tag your partner by pointing to him/her. Your partner connects the first topic to the next topic. Help your partner if he/she has trouble connecting the topics. He/She continues with several sentences until he/she tags you for the next topic. Do this activity for the topics *weather/nature/TV show/town/shopping*. You can also do this with a group of four other students.

Play "Musical Topics" with several other students. To play, each student writes down five topics on individual 3 × 5 cards; then the students give the cards to the "DJ" of the group. The DJ draws a card, announces the topic, and plays music by humming or using a radio, iPod, phone, etc. While the music is playing, students talk in pairs about the topic until the DJ stops the music. After the DJ draws the second topics, each student, working in a pair, tries to verbally connect the two topics in different ways. Partners give each other a point for successful connections. If one student cannot make a connection, the other may step in and receive an extra point. The game goes on until the DJ runs out of cards. The student with the higher score wins.

Practice speaking about multiple topics by working with four other students. Form a circle. The first student picks the first topic and says one sentence about it. Moving clockwise around the circle, two more students say different sentences about the topic. Listen to each person's sentence to hear other ideas for speaking about the topic. When it is the fourth student's turn, he/she says a sentence to link the first topic to the second. Then the next three students take turns saying sentences about the second topic. Continue this pattern (three students say topic sentences, one says a linking sentence) until all topics have been used. Practice this activity with the topics of *town, job, technology.*

Other strategy suggested by the teacher or peers:

Spontaneous Speaking

Purpose: To narrate or supply one side of a dialogue for a previously unseen TV show, movie, or Internet clip (spontaneous speaking)
Level: Advanced
Speaking: Presentational
Grouping: Groups of two
Form: Figure 3.20 Spontaneous Speaking Assessment Form (page 127)

Full Procedure

Show the student pairs a previously unseen clip from a TV show, movie, or Internet video without the sound (Tuttle, 2007). The clip should be one with many actions and different scenes/images; it does not need to be in the target language. Do not use clips that show English words. Instruct Student 1 to provide either the narration or one side of the dialogue. If he/she does the dialogue, he/she can talk for any character or characters on the screen. After you say, "Start," Student 1 begins to narrate or gives the dialogue for a minute and a half. Student 2 listens and makes a slash (/) for each sentence that is comprehensible and meaningful for the situation. Student 2 only marks complete sentences, not individual words or phrases, such "the store" or "big red." At the end of the minute and a half, Student 2 tells Student 1 the number of sentences and any major mistakes in speaking. He/She can also tell Student 1 what he/she could have said. Student 1 records these in the "Improve" section of the form. Then the students reverse roles. The learners look over the suggestions for improvements, practice using them, and reassess themselves using the same clip or additional reassessment topics.

Implementing Formative Feedback

After you collect this assessment form, monitor each student's baseline. Scan the papers to identify those students who were already proficient according to your predetermined criteria or have become proficient due to peer assessment. Share the *Formative Strategies* with those students who have a learning gap in this area. Those students select a new strategy, practice that strategy with random topics over several class periods, and then are reassessed using the original topic.

Extension

Next, the students can collectively narrate the show. Student 1 says a sentence and then Student 2 says the next. Also, they can do a running commentary on the clip as sports commentators would, using phrases such as "What a horrible dress she has!" or "She looks mad!" Likewise, students can ask questions of the characters' actions, such as "Why did you put your books under the sink?" or "Who are you calling?"

Speaking Topics
First clip: *Blossom* (tinyurl.com/BlossomTV, 2:30-4:00)
Second clip: *Lucy* (tinyurl.com/fatv2, 3:40-5:10)
Third clip: Any TV show, movie, or Internet clip can be used *without sound* as long as it contains many actions and does not have any information (signs, products) in English.

Formative Strategies for Spontaneous Speaking

For the narration, figure out what the people are doing or what they are talking about. Then say the action and a detail, such as "The tall man talks to the woman. She is happy. She wants to kiss the man. . . . " Add in any details that seem logical. Practice with a TV clip.

When there is little action taking place in the clip, narrate by describing in more detail the place, the people, the objects, the weather, etc. You may say, "The desk is big. It is made of wood. The chair is very old." Practice with a TV clip.

To practice narrating, take your picture verb flashcards (picture on one side and target language on the other side), turn them to the picture side, and pick the first twenty cards. Think of a topic such as *school* and use each verb, one at a time, to say meaningful sentences about school. Incorporate each new verb into your story as quickly as possible.

Practice with another student who wants to improve in the area of spontaneous speaking. Narrate the TV, movie, or Internet clip. If you cannot think of anything to say, your partner will point to a specific person, object, on the screen for you to talk about. Practice with a TV clip.

For both narration and giving dialogue, give the major characters names so that you do not have to say "the man" or "the woman" over and over again. Identify the person as "good" or "bad" or use other characteristics and then tell what such a person would do. For example, "Saul does not like Victor. Victor likes Saul's girlfriend." Practice with a TV clip.

For both narration and giving dialogue, describe the emotions you see and what may have caused those emotions. For example, you may say, "Pam is

FIGURE 3.20 Spontaneous Speaking Assessment Form

Assessment: _____ Date: _____

	Student 1	Student 2
Clip		
Number: Narration		
Number: Dialogue		
Improve		
New strategy		
Practice topics		
Reassess		
Number (original topic)		

happy because she receives money" or "Pam is sad because she is not with Jack." Practice this strategy with a TV clip.

For narration and dialogue, use short sentences since the scenes change quickly. For example, you say, "She is mad. She runs out of the room." Practice this strategy with a TV clip.

For either narration or dialogue, think of a situation that people, real or on TV, talk about and incorporate that into your dialogue. If the show takes place in an office, think of classroom- or office-related actions, objects, sentences, and questions. Incorporate them into talking about this show. Practice this strategy with a TV clip.

Change the video clip to another genre by providing the dialogue. For example, you can change a comedy into a soap opera by using the emotional words that characters in a soap opera would say if they were in the given situation. Watch a clip and change it to a Police show where each person is questioning each other for information.

For practicing the dialogue, pretend your left hand is one person and your right hand is another person. Have your hands talk to each other. Open your hand as you ask a question or make a statement. Close the hand as you answer or react to the other person. See how quickly your hands can open and close. Practice this strategy with a TV clip.

Practice a dialogue with another student who wants to improve in the area of spontaneous speaking. You can take on the role of one of the main characters while your partner becomes another main character. If the main character interacts with anyone who is not the other main character, then your partner takes on that role. Practice this strategy with a TV clip.

Practice giving dialogue with another student by pretending to be two objects in the scene that comment on the main characters. For example, a sofa might say to a chair, "Tom and Jean are sitting in chairs, not on me. They are mad at each other." Or a chair might respond, "John is fat. He eats too much."

Practice a dialogue with another student by pretending to do the actions on the TV clip as you say the dialogue. Add in other actions and comment on them. For example, you and your partner can pretend to be a husband and wife. As one of you acts out putting dishes in the dishwasher, you can complain about all the dirty dishes and say you want to eat out more.

Other strategy suggested by the teacher or peers:

References

Ainsworth, L., & Viegut, D. (2006). *Common formative assessments*. Thousand Oaks, CA: Corwin Press.

American Council for the Teaching of Foreign Languages. (1998). *ACTFL performance guidelines for K–12 learners*. Yonkers, NY: American Council on the Teaching of Foreign Languages.

American Council for the Teaching of Foreign Languages. (1999). *ACTFL revised proficiency guidelines—Speaking*. Yonkers, NY: American Council on the Teaching of Foreign Languages. Retrieved March 11, 2010, from www.sil.org/lingualinks/languagelearning/OtherResources/ACTFLProficiencyGuidelines/contents.htm

American Council for the Teaching of Foreign Languages. (2010). *ACTFL position statement: The use of the target language in the classroom*. Retrieved October 10, 2010, from www.actfl.org

American Council for the Teaching of Foreign Languages. (n.d.). *Integrated performance assessment (IPA) manual*. Retrieved March 11, 2010, from www.actfl.org/i4a/pages/index.cfm?pageid=3565

Bailey, K. M. (2005). *Practical English language teaching: Speaking*. New York, NY: McGraw-Hill.

Bivens, T. B. (n.d.). LinguaFolio: A tool for reflective learning and student self-assessment. *Slideshare*. Retrieved July 2, 2011 from www.slideshare.net/tbiv0105/linguafolio-presentation-for-ncvps

Black, P., & Jones, J. (2006). Formative assessment and the learning and teaching of MFL: Sharing the language learning road map with learners. *Language Learning Journal, 34*, 4–9. Retrieved March 18, 2010, from Academic Premier Database.

Black, P., & Wiliam, D. (1998). Inside the black box: Raising standards through classroom assessment. *Phi Delta Kappa International, 80*(2), 139–148. Retrieved July 30, 2005, from www.pdkintl.org/kappan/kbla9810.htm

Blaz, D. (2001). *A collection of performance tasks and rubrics: Foreign languages*. Larchmont, NY: Eye On Education.

Breiner-Sanders, K. E., Lowe, P. Jr., Miles, J., & Swender, E. (2000). ACTFL proficiency guidelines—Speaking (Revised 1999). *Foreign Language Annals, 33*, 13–18.

Brookhart, S. M. (2008). *How to give effective feedback to your students*. Alexandria, VA: Association for Supervision and Curriculum Development.

Buttner, A. (2007). *Activities, games and assessment strategies for the foreign language classroom*. Larchmont, NY: Eye On Education.

Center for Advanced Research on Language Acquisition. (2010). Acronyms for the basic differences. *Spanish grammar strategies*. Retrieved October 19, 2010, from www.carla.umn.edu/strategies/sp_grammar/strategies/form/serandestar/whentouse.html

Center for Applied Linguistics. (2010). *Testing/assessment*. Retrieved March 12, 2010, from www.cal.org/topics/ta/oralassess.html

Center for Language Teaching Advancement. (2008). *MSU's SOPI testing program.* Retrieved March 12, 2010, from celta.msu.edu/assessment/sopiTesting.pdf

Chamot, A. U. (2004). Issues in language learning strategy research and teaching. *Electronic Journal of Foreign Language Teaching, 1*(1), 14–26. Retrieved March 11, 2009, from e-flt.nus.edu.sg/v1n12004/chamot.htm

Clarke, S. (2005). *Formative assessment in action: Weaving the elements together.* London, UK: Hodder-Murray.

Dann, T. (2009). *3rd can do statements.* West Des Moines Community Schools. Retrieved March 11, 2009, from https://staff.wdmcs.org/sites/Portal/FLES/Language%20Portfolio/3rd%20can%20do%20statements.pdf

Fall, T., Adair-Hauck, B., & Gilsan, E. (2007). Assessing students' oral proficiency: A case for online testing. *Foreign Language Annals 40*(3), 377–406. Retrieved March 25, 2010, from Academic Premier Database.

Foreign Language Program of Studies. (2004). Level 2 speaking tasks: Analytic rubric. *Fairfax county public schools—PALS: Performance assessment for language students.* Retrieved March 30, 2010, from www.fcps.edu/DIS/OHSICS/forlang/PALS/rubrics/pdfs/Level%202%20Speaking%20Tasks%20Analytic%20Rubric.pdf

Hall, K., & Burke, W. M. (2003). *Making formative assessment work: Effective practice in the primary classroom.* Berkshire, England: Open University Press.

Hattie, J. (1999, August). *Influences on student learning.* Inaugural lecture: Professor of Education, University of Auckland.

Heritage, M. (2007). Formative assessment: What do teachers need to know and do? *Phi Delta Kappa, 89*(2), 140–145, from Academic Search Premier.

Howell, R., Patton, S., & Deoitte, M. (2008). *Understanding response to intervention: A practical approach to systemic implementation.* Bloomington, IL: Solution Tree.

Hunter, M. (1976). Teacher competency: Problem, theory and practice. *Theory into Practice, 15*(2), 162–171.

Jefferson Parish Public Schools. (n.d.). *Quilt stage III prompt student responses.* Retrieved November 11, 2007, from www.jppss.k12.la.us/teachers/quilt/QUILT%20Stage%20III.ppt

Krashen, S. (2003). *Explorations in language acquisition and use.* Portsmouth, VA: Heinemann.

Langrehr, J. (2001). *Teaching our children to think.* Bloomington, IN: Solution Tree.

Leahy, S., Lyon, C., Thompson, M., & Wiliam, D. (2005). Classroom assessment minute by minute, day by day. *Educational Leadership, 63*(3), 19–24.

Lipton, L., & Wellman, B. (1998). *Pathways to understanding: Patterns and practice in the learning-focused classroom.* Guilford, VT: Pathways Publishing.

LTI, The ACTFL Testing Office. (n.d.). ACTFL oral proficiency interview (OPI) application for NJ teacher certification. Retrieved March 12, 2010, from www.languagetesting.com/download/NJ_State_OPI_ApplicationWL.doc

Marzano, R. J. (2000). *Transforming classroom grading.* Alexandria, VA: Association for Supervision and Curriculum Development.

Marzano, R. J. (2004). *Building background knowledge for academic achievement.* Alexandria, VA: Association for Supervision and Curriculum Development.

Marzano, R. J. (2007). *The art and science of teaching.* Alexandria, VA: Association for Supervision and Curriculum Development.

McTighe, J., & O'Connor, K. (2006). Seven practices for effective learning. *Educational Leadership, 63*(3), 10–17.

Moss, C. M., & Brookhart, S. M. (2009). *Advancing formative assessment in every classroom*. Alexandria, VA: Association for Supervision and Curriculum Development.

National Standards in Foreign Language Education. (1996). *Standards for foreign language learning: Preparing for the 21st century*. Retrieved March 11, 2010, from www.actfl.org/files/public/execsumm.pdf

Office for Standards in Education, Children's Services and Skills. (2008, July 4). Speaking is the weak link in language teaching. *Education (14637073)*. Retrieved March 25, 2010, from Academic Search Premier database.

Hadley, A. O. (2001). *Teaching language in context*. Boston, MA: Heinle & Heinle.

Popham, W. J. (2008). *Transformative assessment*. Alexandria, VA: Association for Supervision and Curriculum Development.

Primary National Strategy. (2004). *Part 5: Feedback on learning*. Retrieved November 10, 2007, from www.standards.dfes.gov.uk/primary/features/resources/primary/pns_landt052104a4l_s5.pdf

Salt, M. (2010, February 24). Speed dating in the MFL classroom. *Languages and learning*. Retrieved March 27, 2010, from amandasalt.blogspot.com/2010/02/speed-dating-in-mfl-classroom.html

Sandrock, P. (2008). Integrated performance assessment. Retrieved March 12, 2010, from depts.washington.edu/mellwa/Events/20081105/sandrock_ipa_handout.pdf

Silver, H. F., Strong, R. W., and Perini, M. J. (2007). *The strategic teacher: Selecting the right research-based strategy for every lesson*. Upper Saddle River, N.J.: Pearson Education.

Stiggins, R. J. (2007). *An introduction to student-involved assessment for learning* (5th ed.). Upper Saddle River, NJ: Pearson Education.

Tomlinson, C. A., & McTighe, J. (2006). *Integrating differentiated instruction & understanding by design: Connecting content and kids*. Alexandria, VA: Association for Supervision and Curriculum.

Tuttle, H. G. (1975). Using visual material in the foreign language classroom. *ACFTL Learning Resources*, 2(5), 9–13.

Tuttle, H. G. (1982). Spanish airline simulation. *Spanish today*, XV(2), 5–6.

Tuttle, H. G. (1994). *Restructuring education for quality learning: From ideas to action*. Ithaca, NY: Epilog Visions.

Tuttle, H. G. (2007, November 15). *Livening up foreign language. TechLearning*. Retrieved March 26, 2010, from www.techlearning.com/article/8110

Tuttle, H. G. (2009). *Formative assessment: Responding to your students*. Larchmont, NY: Eye On Education.

Tuttle, H. G. (2010). Modern language learning success through formative assessment. *Language Association Journal of the New York State Association of Foreign Language Teachers*, 61(2), 12–13.

Tuttle, H. G. (2010). *Success student writing through formative assessment*. Larchmont, NY: Eye On Education.

University of Minnesota's Center for Advanced Research on Language Acquisition. (2009). *Developing speaking and writing tasks for second language assessments*. Retrieved March 11, 2010 from www.carla.umn.edu/assessment/MLPA/pdfs/miniguide.pdf

Washburn, N., & Christianson, K. (1995). Teaching conversation strategies through pair-taping. *TESL Reporter*, 29(2), 41–52.

White, E. (2009). Student perspectives of peer assessment for learning in a public speaking course. *Asian EFL Journal, 33.* Retrieved October 23, 2010, from www .slideshare.net/ewhite/student-perspectives-of-peer-assessment-for-learning-in-a-public-speaking-course

Wiggins, G. (1998). *Educative assessment: Designing assessments to inform and improve student performance.* San Francisco, CA: Jossey-Bass.

Willis, J. (2006). *Research-based strategies to ignite student learning.* Alexandria, VA: Association for Supervision and Curriculum Development.

Online Sources

Audacity (audacity.sourceforge.net/)

Flickr (www.flickr.com)

Google Images. (www.google.com)

Pbworks (pbworks.com)

ProProfs (www.proprofs.com/flashcards/cloud.php)

Quia (www.quia.com/shared/search)

Tuttle's Education with Technology blog (www.eduwithtechn.wordpress.com)

Voki (www.voki.com)

Webspiration (www.mywebspiration.com)

Zoomerang (www.zoomerang.com)